Be a Party Plan

SUPERSTAR

Build a $100,000-a-Year
Direct Selling Business from Home

Mary Christensen

AMACOM

American Management Association

New York • Atlanta • Brussels • Chicago • Mexico City • San Francisco
Shanghai • Tokyo • Toronto • Washington, D.C.

This publication is designed to provide accurate and authoritative information in regard to the subject matter covered. It is sold with the understanding that the publisher is not engaged in rendering legal, accounting, or other professional service. If legal advice or other expert assistance is required, the services of a competent professional person should be sought.

Library of Congress Cataloging-in-Publication Data

Christensen, Mary, 1951–
    Be a party plan superstar : build a $100,000-a-year direct selling business
        from home / Mary Christensen.
        p. cm.
    Includes index.
    ISBN-13: 978-0-8144-1651-8 (pbk.)
    ISBN-10: 0-8144-1651-9 (pbk.)
1. Home parties (Marketing) 2. Direct selling. 3. Home-based businesses.
        I. Title.
    HF5438.25.C5125 2011
    658.8'72—dc22
                                2010014278

About AMA
American Management Association (www.amanet.org) is a world leader in talent development, advancing the skills of individuals to drive business success. Our mission is to support the goals of individuals and organizations through a complete range of products and services, including classroom and virtual seminars, Webcasts, Webinars, podcasts, conferences, corporate and government solutions, business books, and research. AMA's approach to improving performance combines experiential learning—learning through doing—with opportunities for ongoing professional growth at every step of one's career journey.

Printing number

10 9 8 7 6 5 4 3 2 1

Contents

Acknowledgments

THANKS TO MY WONDERFUL EDITOR, Ellen Kadin, and the team at AMACOM for your support; my agent, Ed Knappman of New England Publishing Associates, for your encouragement; Wayne Christensen for your superb editing; and party plan superstars around the world for your inspiration.

With love to my mother, Ida, for your strength, and my father, Jack, for making me strong.

To Wayne, Nikki, David, Tiffany, Matt, Samantha, Brayden, Paige, Trinity, Jett, Dane, Beki, Frances, Jim, Gordon, Gary, Bev, Geoff, Catherine, Brittany, Callum, Matt, Sonia, Grace, James, Jenny, Mike, Tayla, Ella, Tristan, Caroline, George, Irian, Wayne, Cayce, Tiffany, Mason, Marvon, Kelly, Izak, Kaydence, Brad, Jacqui, Mike, Ross, Marilyn, Jan, Ray, Doug, Dori, Ed, Shirley, John, Susan, Herm, Louise, Mary, Angela, Bill, Muriel, Nancy, JT, Bob, Pauline, Brian, Rick, and Rena for enriching my life.

There's No Business Like Show Business

PARTY PLAN SELLING IS THE PERFECT VEHICLE for personal and financial growth. Whatever your current circumstances are financially or otherwise, you don't have to settle for less than you want when you can have it all as a star of your own "show business."

Party plan is a business model that anyone can follow. As an independent business entrepreneur, you partner with a corporation, which takes care of the back end of the business (including the products, marketing, administration, and technical support) so that you can focus on the front-line activities that will drive your income.

No matter what you call them—parties, shows, classes, presentations, group consultations, workshops, gatherings, celebrations, experiences, or demonstrations—parties are the perfect way to build a business.

Whether you currently work inside or outside the home, a

party plan business could be your route out of debt and into financial freedom. You can work full-time, part-time, or in your spare time and still hit the big time.

Why wait for customers to come to you when you can bring your business into their living rooms? Most business owners would swap their souls to stand in front of a captive audience in the warm, friendly environment of their customers' homes.

If you're ready to start calling the shots on your life, this book will teach you how to build a successful party plan business from the ground up. If you're already a party planner, you will learn how to catapult your business to the highest levels of your compensation plan.

You will create income for today with higher sales, income for tomorrow with more bookings, and income forever by empowering others to become successful party plan entrepreneurs.

The sooner you start, the sooner you can start enjoying all the rewards that will come your way as a party plan superstar:

* Family first
* Financial security
* Friendships
* Flexibility
* Freedom
* Freebies
* Fun

If you are a direct seller or multilevel marketer and your company doesn't have a traditional party plan structure, you can still incorporate party plan concepts into your business. My strategies will help you communicate effectively with one, ten, or one hundred business prospects. The strategies will add pizzazz to your business presentations and fire up your meetings, training seminars, and product launches.

Many direct selling, multilevel marketing, and network marketing companies are embracing party plan concepts to reach a wider audience. When companies stage opportunity nights or business seminars, they're employing party plan techniques. The only difference is the product they're promoting is the business.

If your product lends itself to demonstration, display, education, or experience, it makes sense to market it to groups. Why talk to one person when you could talk to ten?

If it's new, unique, or innovative, the sooner you establish market share, the harder you will make it for competitors to gain a foothold.

If you're confident that your product offers better quality or better value than anything that's available through stores, telemarketers, or online retailers, party plan is an effective way to spread the word.

I stumbled into party plan as a young mom. I was raising my family and working as an elementary school teacher. Every weekday I had to leave my baby son and two-year-old daughter with a babysitter, while I was at school. When they were safely tucked into bed at night, I prepared lessons for my class of nine-year-olds. Weekends were a juggling act of household chores and family time. I often dropped the ball.

My children deserved better, but not working wasn't an option. The bills had to be paid. When I saw an advertisement that offered "Work from Home," the lightbulb flashed and I picked up the phone. Less than eight hours later a stylish woman was sitting at my kitchen table. She interviewed me for all of thirty minutes, and to my delight, I got the job.

Not exactly the job I had expected, but it sounded exciting enough for me to leave my teaching career behind to sell skin care and color products as an independent party plan consultant. That meant swapping a teacher's salary and benefits for a compensation plan and a promise that the harder I worked, the more I would earn. I seized on party plan as a second chance to be the mom my children deserved.

My sponsor happened to be in the right place at the right time when I came along. She left the business soon afterward and I never heard from her again, so her personal impact on me was small but the impact she made on my life was huge.

With no experience in sales or beauty (as a working mom, I barely found time to wash my face let alone follow a full skin care routine) I set about learning the business. Just as I had stumbled *into* party plan, I stumbled many times after.

My Starter Kit was a beauty case that contained an assortment of demonstration products, including one solitary eye shadow duo. If I wanted more eyeshadows I would have to buy them. For my first few weeks in business, I had to persuade my customers that shimmering turquoise and white eyes were the hottest new look. I still cringe when I recall my first efforts as a makeup artist.

But I believe that everything is hard until it's easy, so I began building my demonstration products and my knowledge until I could offer my customers a wider choice of products—and better advice.

I was not an overnight superstar, but I was willing to work and willing to learn, and that paid off for me. Every change I made was a small step forward, and as long as I took more steps forward than backward I felt as though I was making progress. I learned that if things weren't working for me, I had to change, and not expect others to change. But the single greatest lesson I learned was that it takes courage, not confidence, to build a business.

I changed my life through my party plan business. I changed my family's life. We have the lifestyle we want—and the money to pay for it. What more could we ask for?

And that's why, more than twenty-five years on, when I'm asked to explain what gives party plan its magic, I can offer a dozen reasons:

1. The few dollars you invest in a Starter Kit will typically be matched, in products and business supplies, many times over by the corporation you choose to partner with. I can't think of any other investment that doubles or triples (or more) in value from day one.

2. The Starter Kit is just the beginning of the support you will enjoy. Because the corporation has a stake in your success, it will do all it can to help you succeed, from training and recognition to marketing, technological, and administrative support.

3. The compensation plan (which is sometimes called the reward plan, marketing plan, or career plan) provides a simple, step-by-step blueprint for success. Decide where you want to take your business and the plan will guide you there.

4. Although you're in business for yourself, you are never *by* yourself. Your sponsor and up-line managers will support you to the best of their abilities. Not least because they will be paid on your results. If you're not earning, neither are they.

5. You will earn as you learn. Enthusiasm counts more than experience, and you can practice on friends, family, and neighbors to gain confidence and skills.

6. It's a win/win business. In return for helping you launch your business by hosting your first parties, your friends and family will be rewarded with free products and buying privileges. Those same rewards will encourage *their* friends to book, and more bookings will flow from those parties. The generous host reward program will help you create ever-widening circles of business contacts.

7. You will enjoy the significant tax breaks that are available to any business entrepreneur who works from home,

SUPERSTAR SECRET

An exciting discovery you will make when you review the compensation plan is that it has a multilevel structure. The majority of party plan companies have a multilevel marketing compensation plan that allows you to earn income in three different ways:

1. Commission on your personal sales. The higher your sales each month, the higher your commission will be. The more parties you do, the greater your sales will be.

2. Training bonuses on the sales of people you introduce (sponsor or recruit) to the business. These bonuses are your reward for sharing your business and skills.

3. Additional bonuses on the sales of those who become managers. The industry calls them "breakaway managers" and the more breakaway managers you develop, the more you can earn.

even as you're establishing your business. If you can show a clear intent to make a profit, even your start-up costs could be deductible.

8. You decide when, where, and with whom you work. No more subsidizing lazy coworkers, working unpaid overtime, or pleading for a raise. You can kiss petty office politics good-bye and surround yourself with like-minded people who will inspire you to be the best you can be.

9. You will keep most of what you earn. It costs very little to run a party plan business. You don't have to pay staff, lease premises, or invest in inventory, marketing, and business supplies. Your expenses will be minimal because you will pay only for products and supplies you sell or consume.

10. You will be recognized for your efforts. Every step of your progress will be acknowledged and every milestone will be applauded.

11. Once you have mastered the skills of party plan, you only have to keep applying them to take your business all the way to the top.

12. Best of all, you will control your destiny. If you're willing to work and willing to learn, you can live a lifestyle most people only dream about.

Why settle for being a cog in an increasingly rusty corporate wheel, with zero appreciation, control, or security, when you can own your own business and choose when you work, with whom you work, and what you earn?

If you're a woman, why accept inequalities that are rife in the workplace, such as being paid seventy-seven cents for the exact same job a man is paid one dollar to do just because of your gender? (*Source:* U.S. Census.)

Why waste years climbing the corporate ladder only to find the ladder's leaning against the wrong wall? Only fifteen women currently head Fortune 500 corporations, and only twenty-eight Fortune 1000 companies have women in the top job. These statistics are damning evidence that the odds are stacked heavily against women who choose corporate career paths. (*Source:* CNNMoney.com.)

Why sacrifice your family life to earn a dollar when party plan empowers you to stay true to your family-first values and earn income at the same time?

When you control your income, you control your life, and for women especially a party plan business tops the list of ideal career options.

My party plan business transformed my life, and your party plan business can transform yours. There are no shortcuts, but this book is packed with strategies that accelerated my success, including many of my exclusive party plan superstar secrets. All you have to do is implement them to gain an edge over your competitors. By sharing these strategies with everyone you sponsor into the business, you will compound your advantage many times over.

No more waiting in the wings of your life. It's time to step on up and make your party the greatest show on earth.

PART ONE

Who Wants to Be a Superstar?

CHAPTER 1

Light Your Fire

WHAT I LOVE MOST ABOUT PARTY PLAN is that it empowers us to live by different rules. What we set our hearts on, we can have. We don't have to wonder, "Can I afford it?" as workers on fixed incomes do. With no limit on what we can earn, there's no limit on what we can have.

Your first step to firing up your party plan business is to find a goal worth working for. Small goals have all the firepower of a dead battery. Fully charged goals will keep you energized and excited even after you've just hung up from your fourth "no" in a row.

Set a goal that is so powerful it eclipses every disappointment, doubt, doomsayer, or distraction that you encounter along the way. If debt has you trapped behind the starting gate, make a goal to set yourself free. Imagine how you will feel when you pay off your credit cards, release your student loan, or live in a mortgage-free home.

If you are miserable at work, start planning your exit strategy. You deserve better than deadbeat coworkers or a boss who talks to you only when he wants something. If your job is draining the sap out of you, no matter how much money you earn, what's the point?

If you are spending the best years of your children's life at work, although your heart is telling you that no way, after they have left home, will you wish you had spent a single second less with them while they were growing up, set the wheels in motion to bring your work home.

With a party plan business you can have the best of both worlds—be the mom your kids deserve *and* be a successful business entrepreneur.

The easiest option you have in life is to stick with what you know, snug in your comfort zone. But the price of playing it safe is high. By following the same tired routine day after day, or clinging to a job that has passed its use-by date, you may be giving up your chance to live an amazing life.

Every party plan superstar I know is driven by a passion for improving her life. Some of their stories are certain to inspire you to find a goal that you can be passionate about.

Brittany's goal is a cow:

"I grew up on a farm. Every morning I woke up to see our two pet cows in the paddock outside my window. When we married, my husband and I moved closer to town. I love having my own home but when I open the blinds every morning, all I see is our neighbor's fence. My goal is to save enough for a deposit on land farther out of town, so that one day we can build our dream home on it. I want my kids to grow up in a home that has land around it. I want them to see cows grazing outside their window. I want them to have the same wonderful childhood my parents gave me."

Grace's goal is teeth:

"I am married to the most amazing man. We met at school and married as soon as we graduated. He is the best husband ever. We have three beautiful children and he works hard to make sure our family has everything we need. But he never smiles. He wasn't smiling when I met him and I thought he was just being mysterious. But he's not smiling in our prom photos, and he's not smiling in our wedding photos. And that's because he's ashamed of his teeth. He would have so much more confidence if he could have his teeth fixed, but everything he earns goes to our house and kids. There is never anything left when all the bills are paid. My goal is to earn enough money to be able to hand my husband a check and say, 'This is for your new teeth.' "

Ella's goal is a second honeymoon:

"When we got married, my parents' wedding gift to us was a honeymoon in Hawaii. It was the most wonderful week of my life. That was nine years ago and we have never been away together since. My goal is to buy two tickets to Hawaii so we can spend our tenth wedding anniversary reliving our honeymoon."

When you couple a meaningful goal with a realistic deadline you will move mountains to make it happen.

Long-term goals encourage procrastination. When you can't see the prize, there's less incentive to keep moving toward it when the going gets tough. What difference will it make to do nothing today if it's going to take ten years to reach your goal?

Short-term goals are powered by urgency. No matter what

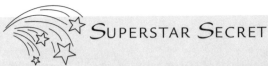

SUPERSTAR SECRET

Start every year by setting a goal that makes your eyes shine, a goal so powerful that you can feel your heart beat faster every time you think about it. If you don't experience an immediate, emotional, instinctive response when thinking about your goal, dig deep until you find one that does set you on fire.

challenges you encounter, you'll find it easier to stay focused if you can see the finish line. With the payoff for your efforts in your sights, you will find the strength to forge ahead.

When you find a goal that makes your pulse race, paste pictures on your wall or screensaver to remind you every day why you're making calls, following up on leads, and driving ten miles across town. Let the picture of your new kitchen, dream car, RV, family vacation, or new teeth keep you energized and excited.

If you have to run your business from the corner of the kitchen table or after you've spent eight hours at your regular job, or when your toddler's taking a nap, don't let that stop you. If you don't have the best support in the world, don't let that be your excuse. You can't make excuses and progress at the same time.

To achieve true happiness, you have to be prepared to move beyond your comfort zone and pursue what you truly want in life. So think big. There is no reason to think small when you have all the resources of your corporate partner at your disposal. Nor is there any sense in playing it small when you have the ability to turn your goals into reality.

CHAPTER 2

Believe It to Achieve It

MORE THAN FIFTEEN MILLION AMERICANS, an average of one person in every ten households, are direct sellers. Five million of them choose to operate their businesses by party plan, and the overwhelming majority of party planners are women (98 percent, according to the Direct Selling Association).

The reason is simple: Women are born with every skill needed to succeed as self-employed entrepreneurs. Women have a natural ability to:

* Share
* Network
* Nurture
* Organize
* Multitask

✻ **SHARING IS IN OUR DNA.** Women are constantly talking, recommending, and swapping stories about the things we love. When we see a wonderful movie, read an amazing book, or discover a new recipe we immediately think, "My sister Frances would love this" or, "This would be perfect for my friend Kate." We're comfortable seeking the advice of friends and we trust their ideas, suggestions, and recommendations.

Even the most inexperienced salesperson knows that selling is not about facts, figures, and statistics. Selling is about sharing credible stories and testimonials so that others can benefit from our knowledge and experiences. As soon as we learn when it's time to stop talking and start listening we shine in the communication department.

✻ **WOMEN INSTINCTIVELY NETWORK.** There's no training required when it comes to meeting others. We find it practically impossible to stand beside someone for a few minutes and *not* start talking. We can strike up conversations, even with strangers, in seconds. You will never hear a man saying to the person next in line, "I love your shoes!"

✻ **MENTORING COMES NATURALLY.** Women are nurturers by nature, and that's how a party plan business grows. We get what *we* want by helping others get what *they* want. Growing a party plan business is much like raising kids. Our prime responsibility as parents is to raise our children to become independent adults. It's the same role we play in our party plan business when we mentor our consultants to become independent business owners.

✻ **WOMEN ARE BORN ORGANIZERS.** You don't need a degree in business management to run a business. I graduated from college, founded successful businesses, headed two party plan corporations, and served as president of two national associations. I'm sharing this with you for one reason. And that's because I didn't learn management skills in any of those roles. I learned them from organizing my life, my home, and my family. If you can run a home, raise a family, and organize your life, you are fully equipped to run a multimillion-dollar business.

   * **MULTITASKING IS OUR GOD-GIVEN GIFT.** We thrive on our superpowers. We can clean the house, plan a shopping trip, and care for our children all at the same time. We check our e-mail as we make calls, and plan the next day's schedule as we prepare a meal. We do it by setting priorities and tackling what needs to be done. Building a party plan business involves juggling many balls—booking, coaching, presenting, ordering, servicing, prospecting, sponsoring, and mentoring. Women can do it all because we were created that way.

   Women and business make a perfect match. The evidence is in the statistics: According to government sources, women own more than ten million privately held businesses in America, representing sales of over $2.3 trillion annually (see http://www.score.org/women_stats.html).

   But the outlook for most small businesses is not entirely rosy. The failure rate is high, and lack of cash cripples most of them. The up-front capital needed to start a business is just the beginning of the expense. Businesses need ongoing cash flow to sustain them. Fixed overheads can topple a business when customer traffic is slow because of seasonal cycles or economic fluctuations. With the odds so heavily stacked against small businesses, all women should seriously consider how much risk they are prepared to take to own one.

   That you won't have to invest cash in your party plan business makes it a standout business choice. Why risk your own capital when there is a long line of party plan corporations only too eager to be your backer?

   Isolation is a challenge that many small-business owners

encounter. Going it alone can be tough. Women thrive on support, and many small businesses are solo operations.

I recently visited a day spa and started chatting to the vibrant young woman who owned it. She had always dreamed of having a business and had done everything she could to make it happen. It turned out that the one challenge she hadn't factored in when she started her business was the loneliness. She had no business partners, no coworkers, and no support system. I couldn't help but feel sorry that during her small-business search she hadn't investigated party plan, where she would have had all the support she craved.

If neither cash nor support is an issue, what could possibly hold you back? If you're a woman, you are most likely overestimating the challenge and underestimating yourself. Think about how we look at ourselves in a mirror: We get as close as we can so that we can scrutinize every imperfection. You have to move on from self-doubt and uncertainty to realize your true potential in life.

There is no "Reserved" sign on success in party plan. Especially when it comes to gender. The path has been well traveled by millions of women who have transformed their lives through their party plan businesses. Every one of them has lit the path that will guide you on your journey.

If you want it, and you're prepared to work for it, you can have it.

PART TWO

Building Your Business

CHAPTER 3

Master the Art of Selling

A PARTY PLAN BUSINESS IS ABOUT SHARING the products you love, but you are paid only when someone buys them, and in any language that spells selling.

So let's take the fear factor out of selling, especially the sticky parts, such as handling objections and closing the sale. Whether you're selling a product, booking a party host, or signing a new recruit, the principles stay the same. It's only their application that changes.

 SUPERSTAR SECRET

Lose the cue cards, flip charts, and scripted presentations as soon as you can and focus on being yourself. Most of us have our "fake detectors" on high alert. Even if you're trying to be sincere, you are not doing yourself any favors by following a script that someone else has written. You have to make the words your own.

Selling is about connecting. You won't connect with everybody, but that's not your goal. You're looking for people who are perfect for *your* products, party, and business opportunity because *your* products, party, and business opportunity are perfect for them.

The more people you talk to, the more likely it is you'll find them. "No's" are part of the process, and I know party planners who count the no's so they know how close they are to hearing the magic word: yes!

Ask a thousand party plan superstars how they reached the top, and they will all say their success came from being consistent and persistent. Discipline is the essential ingredient in success. There are no shortcuts, magic tricks, or secret formulas. Talking to people is the only way to generate business.

You cannot control other people's decisions. You can only control how many people you reach out to and how well you represent your business. If you match honesty with enthusiasm and treat your prospective customers, hosts, and recruits with respect, you will prevail.

 SUPERSTAR SECRET

Imagine every prospective customer, host, and recruit has a tiny pilot light flickering inside her heart. Your job is to ignite the flame so that your prospects are fired up to place an order, book a party, or sign on as your next consultant.

Each one will have different experiences, circumstances, and ambitions, so you'll have to try different fuels to find one that ignites the fire.

Present the benefits of your products, party, and business in as many different ways as possible. You'll know when you've found the right fuel because you'll see their eyes light up. If you're not seeing the lights go on, switch topics.

Many party planners say the hardest part of the business is learning to handle questions and objections. But don't be unsettled by questions and objections. They reveal what your prospects are thinking.

You have a bigger problem if they are *not* asking questions as you will have absolutely no idea what they're thinking. When you have confidence in your products and your business, you will see objections as an invitation to share more information.

Assume every question is a genuine attempt to find answers. Some questions are leading up to a no, but you have to sort through them to find the yes. If your prospects say yes with unresolved issues hanging in the air, they won't be happy. And guess whom they'll blame? If there isn't a fit between your prospects and your business, don't force it.

Handling Objections

The way *not* to handle objections is to argue. Let's say your prospect says, "I just don't see myself as a salesperson."

If you respond, "You'd be great," you are being insensitive by ignoring a genuine concern.

If your prospect says, "I couldn't do that . . . ," it may be a signal your prospect lacks confidence. Countering with "I'm sure you could!" dismisses her fear with no attempt to address it.

Saying, "It's not selling" is dishonest. If it looks like a duck and quacks like a duck . . .

A simple way to remember how to handle objections is to think of the vowels A, E, I, O, U.

"A" for Agree

Agreeing shows respect for your prospects *and* their concerns. It tells them you're listening! If your prospect says, "I don't see myself as a salesperson," say, "I agree. You don't come across that way at all. Do you want to know why I approached you?"

Now that you're talking about *them,* your prospects will be interested in your answer. The magic word in selling is "because." Try saying, "I approached you because you come across as genuine. The fact that you love the products will always be more credible than a sales pitch." Or you could say, "Because you're fun and this is a fun business."

If you give a genuine compliment *and* respond to their concerns, your prospects will feel flattered that you approached them and, even if they decline, will be happy to hear from you the next time you call.

"E" for Empathy

You can show empathy by saying, "I know how you feel."

If your prospect says, "I'm not sure I can sell," you could say, "I know how you feel. I'd never sold anything before and I wasn't sure I could do it. But once I saw how enthusiastic people were about the products, I got excited. What scares you the most? Is it demonstrating the products or asking for the order?" Your question shows genuine interest.

Or you can say, "We all feel nervous at first. But I promise that does wear off!"

Let's say your prospect says, "I'm too busy."

Your reply could be, "With two kids under the age of five, I imagine you have very little time for yourself. I know how it feels. Both of my kids were under five when I started. But I basically began by selling to friends and family. The extra money has made a huge difference to us."

Or say, "I know how you feel. I was working full-time when I started. Starting small is fine. I did only one party a week at the beginning and I treated what I earned as our family fun money."

When prospects raise issues about not having enough time,

explain any time-saving innovations your company offers. For example, if it sends out personalized newsletters on your behalf, tell prospects about the sales these generate with little effort on your part. If your company ships direct to customers, let your prospects know how much time that saves. Prospects who had parents in the business may not realize how much the business has progressed in a generation.

Someone who has difficulty finding a babysitter will be interested to know that training is available online, on CDs and DVDs, and through Webinars, podcasts, and conference calls. They can access the trainings live, or download them from the corporate training archives at whatever time suits her.

A frequent question you will hear is "How do I learn about it all?" When that happens, say, "Good question. I didn't know very much about selling when I started. We get fantastic training and, for me, learning was the interesting part."

Sometimes people raise an objection to fend off a high-pressure pitch. If you are hearing too many objections, try toning it down a little. Chances are that what you think is enthusiasm others will read as a high-pressure sales pitch. When you're relaxed, your prospects will relax.

Empathy will take you further in this business than trying to convince prospects that their doubts or fears are unfounded.

When I first started my business, I was so nervous my knees shook when I stood up to speak. Someone suggested I go to Toastmasters, an organization that helps people become confident speakers in a supportive clublike environment. I summoned up the courage to go to a meeting.

Ten minutes after walking into the room, I knew two things: One, I would die if I was asked to speak, and two, I was never coming back. This was going to be my first and last experience with Toastmasters.

Everyone in the room was so confident and polished. Where were the people like me who needed help? I sat low in my seat and tried to make myself invisible until I could make my escape.

When the break came, I seized my chance, but before I had a chance to leave, a man walked up to me and said, "I know how you're feeling. The first meeting is tough. But you should know that everyone came here because they needed help. The only difference between you and the rest of us is that we've been to more meetings."

One person's empathy stopped me from making one of the biggest mistakes of my life. By sticking with it, despite my fears, I eventually learned to control my nerves. Joining Toastmasters was one of the best decisions I have made in my life. And to think how close I was to walking away.

"I" for Invite

A lot will be revealed when you invite people to open up to you. The more questions you ask, the more responses you will attract. Treat the process as you would any conversation. You can never go wrong by asking people to talk about their favorite topic: themselves.

Learn to ask specific questions. Let's say you are selling nutritional supplements. If you asked me a general question about my diet, I would most likely say, "I try to take care of myself." That answer takes you on a fast track to nowhere.

If you asked me the one thing I would change about my diet, you take away my wiggle room and it's highly likely that I will confess to eating too much chocolate. Now you have something specific to talk about, and you can even use my answer to build empathy: "My worst habit is soda. If I could kick my soda habit . . ."

By asking specific questions, I guarantee you will get revealing answers: "I'd eat less junk food" or "I'd eat less." Now you know exactly what to say next.

My nominee for worst question of all time is "Would Tuesday or Thursday suit you best?" It's self-serving and so artificial. If you don't respect your customers and prospects, they're not going to respect you!

"O" for Offer Your Concerns

If your prospects are silent, that doesn't mean that they have no questions. It's more likely that they have concerns they're not expressing. Start the ball rolling by offering a few of your own concerns.

Let's say you are approaching a host about becoming a consultant, and you ask if she has any questions. If she says, "I don't think so," and you leave it there, it's game over.

Instead, you could say, "The biggest concern I had was whether I knew enough people. But when I saw what our hosts get for helping me get started, I couldn't wait to call my friends."

You can bet that your prospect is thinking about whether she knows enough people. If a sticking point exists, ignoring it won't make it go away. Once you raise it, you can start working on how to remove it.

Don't be shy about raising potential problems. Many aspiring consultants will have concerns about whether they could master the product knowledge. Reassure them by saying, "The main reservation I had was whether I could learn about every product, but at training I learned to focus on just a few key products and build from there."

There can be a very fine line between a yes and a no. Leaving a prospect's concerns unresolved will diminish your chance of hearing "I'm ready to order," "I could host a party next month," or, even better, "Where do I sign?"

"U" for Use Objections

Make sure the conversation travels in the same direction as your prospect's thought processes. If she says, "How much money do you make?" she is most likely thinking, "How much will I make?" so that's what you talk about.

Talking about your earnings per party will have more meaning than a monthly or annual figure. You should say something like the following:

"I average $500 a party and earn 30 percent of that, or around $150. It's good money."

"I'm still working full-time, so I'm only doing one party a week and earning $500 to $600 a month. But I'm working up to doing three parties so I can quit my other job."

"I average two parties a week and earn around $300 for six to seven hours of work, and that includes preparation time. It works out to about $45 or $50 an hour."

The question "How much does it cost to start?" indicates that your prospect has concerns about the expense. Never say, "I'll get to that part later." Your prospect is already thinking about joining or she wouldn't ask the question.

Answer the question and end it with a commercial: "You pay $149 for the Basic Kit or $299 for the Business Builder Kit. The good news is that you receive at least twice that in products and business supplies so you're ahead from the start."

Respond to Booking Objections

You will almost certainly encounter objections when you're asking for bookings. If you're not hearing objections, you're not approaching enough people.

If you treat the objections as a genuine desire to resolve a sticking point, you will handle them with confidence. You can mix and match these responses to most common objections:

Objection: "I don't need the hassle."

Response: "I can understand that. I have a special program just for my busy hosts. All you have to do is choose a date and make up the guest list. I will mail your invitations for you and bring the refreshments. We even deliver guests' orders directly to them."

Objection: "My house is so small."

Response: "I enjoy doing small parties. I can give everyone extra attention. All we need is a small table, and I have a fold-up one that I can bring."

Or say, "One of my favorite parties is my party-in-a-bag. How it works is I bring a few of our most popular products in a bag and the rest we do from the catalog. It's a little different, there's no mess, and it's a lot of fun."

Or say, "How about bringing your friends to my house? I have everything set up and you still get the host rewards."

Objection: "I'm not interested in having a party right now."

Response: "That's fine. Would you like an invitation to one of my open houses?"

Objection: "I work full-time."

Response: "Have you ever had an at-work party? I give you a basket of products to take to work for a week to show your coworkers. All you have to do is bring it home on Friday and I will collect it from you Saturday morning with any orders. You still qualify for the host rewards."

Objection: "I don't *do* parties."

Response: "I understand. It's not everyone's idea of fun. Have you ever thought about having an open house? It's very relaxed because your friends can come and go as they please and you still get all the host benefits."

Objection: "I'm too busy."

Response: "Kelly told me about how demanding your job is. But it sounds exciting. Can I do anything to help? I'm happy to mail out the invitations for you and I can also bring a plate of goodies. That way you can relax and catch up with your friends without any pressure."

Objection: "I don't think I can do it for a few weeks."

Response: "We can do any date that suits you, but I don't want you to miss out on the extra gifts we have for hosts this month. Is there any chance you can do it sooner?"

Or say, "I have two dates before then that I'm hoping to fill, so if you can possibly book your party sooner, I will give you a special gift [or 10 percent off your order tonight] as a thank-you."

Objection: "I need to check with my friends."

Response: "That's a great idea. Let's pick the best date for you first. We can always change it later, but if your friends are like mine, everyone will suggest a different date and then you'll have to call them all again."

Objection: "I don't think my husband would agree."

Response: "I can understand that. What if I brought along a DVD and popcorn for him and the kids and I promise that we'll be finished before the movie ends?"

Objection: "We're partied out."

Response: "You must hang with a fun crowd. I think everyone's having parties because the rewards are so great. Why should you miss out?"

Handling Difficult Questions

Not all questions will be easy ones. I am sure you have had a customer ask, "What makes your products better than others?"

It may be a valid question, but it could equally be a test. Either way, here's what *not* to do:

* Use general phrases, such as "best quality." Those words are so overused they no longer have any meaning.

* Make exaggerated claims, as in "We are the fastest grow-ing [we pay the most, our products work better than the others]." Extravagant claims are unprofessional and mark you as an overenthusiastic amateur.

* Show blind faith, as in "They are the best!" Unless you've tried every product that is available you can't make such a bold claim.

Your potential customers have to buy you before they will consider buying your products. Think of the times you have walked away from a purchase because you didn't like the sales-person. Think of the times you intended only to browse but ended up buying. That's why you must make your answer per-sonal, for example, "The reason I chose this company is . . ."

If you sell linens, say, "The designs are different from any-thing I've seen in stores and being able to see them in your own home makes a huge difference."

If your products are health related you can simply say, "The products worked for me."

If you sell plastic containers, say, "I think they look a lot more stylish than anything you can buy in stores, and mine have lasted for years so I know they stand the test of time. That's why we offer a lifetime guarantee."

If you have ever had a guest interrupt your presentation to say, "You can buy similar products at [name a store] and cheap-er, too," you will know how frustrating it can be. Keep your cool and say, "They have amazing sales, don't they?" and move on. Treat the comment as a statement, not a question. Remember the golden rule ("Do unto others as you would have others do unto you") and never argue an objection, however unreasonable or mean-spirited it sounds. You might win the battle but I guar-antee you will lose the war.

My first business was selling midpriced skin care products.

At one of my first parties, a guest interrupted me with "I only use [she then named an expensive brand]."

In response, I mumbled something about how good my products were. Big mistake. It was a battle of wits and I lost. Over the next week, I kept going over the conversation in my head and thinking what I would say if it ever happened again.

Sure enough the question came up again, but this time I was ready for it. I smiled at the guest who had just named an expensive brand and said, "Your skin looks fabulous" and moved on. The compliment completely took the wind out of her sails and stopped my antagonist in her tracks.

Staying cool under fire shows more confidence and professionalism than weak protestations, such as "My products are as good."

In challenging situations, it's not what happens but how you respond that counts. Your difficult customer is unlikely to buy much anyway, so why waste your time trying to win her over when you can use your energy more productively on others? What's so great about party plan is that the numbers are always going to be on your side.

The key is to stay relaxed, no matter what the objection is. If a business prospect says, "I want to think it over," it could be a brush-off, but she might reconsider if you play your cards right.

Show confidence by saying, "Of course. It took me a few weeks to make up my mind because I wanted to be sure."

To take the pressure off say, "You are right not to rush into a decision." Then, in a relaxed voice, ask, "Are you concerned about how much time you can commit?"

If she says yes, you have something to work with. You can then say, "I know how you feel. I wasn't sure I could put enough time into building a business while I was working full-time. But the rewards have more than made up for the extra hours I work, and because it's such fun, I don't feel as though I'm working harder."

To try to resolve a prospect's concerns, you could say, "This [book/DVD/CD] helped me answer a few questions I had about the business. You can borrow it if you like. I'm coming back this way next week anyway and I can pick it up then."

A worst-case scenario would be that your prospects were not communicating. If you were interested, wouldn't you have a concern or two?

Time to Close

If you've shown a genuine interest in your guests, answered their questions, and addressed their concerns, you'll know when it's time to close. If you don't end your presentations by asking them to buy, book, or sell, you have wasted your time and theirs.

Closing the sale doesn't have to be complicated. It can be as simple as asking, "Who has already decided what they want?" or, "Who wants to go first?"

Assume guests are ready to order by saying, "Let me take you through the order form." If they're not interested, they'll put the form aside, but you have to make it easy for the ones who *are* interested.

Show the same confidence during your one-on-one time by asking:

"What are you thinking?"

"Do you have any questions?"

"Have you decided what you want to order?"

"I can't wait to see what you've chosen."

When they place an order, make them feel good about their decision. Depending on what you sell, you could say:

For skin care products: "Your skin is going to love you!"

For health products: "You're going to have so much more energy."

For vinyl wall expressions: "I can't wait to see photos of the new nursery. It's going to look fantastic."

There are many ways to close on the business.

The invitation close: "I hope you join. I'd love to work with you."

The assumption close: "Do you need help filling out the agreement?"

The recommendation close: "I think you should do it. You would be a natural."

Or say, "I wouldn't be doing my job if I didn't invite you to join. This is the best job I have ever had and I know you'll think the same. We can even go online right now and get you signed up so you can come to our orientation workshop this Saturday."

Or use the "top-down" close: Work your way down through each of your offers, starting by inviting guests to join. If they say no, invite them to host a presentation. If they decline, ask for the order. Who could possibly say no to you three times in a row?

Once you have closed, say nothing more until the guest responds. You may talk yourself out of a sale, booking, or business appointment by chatting while they are trying to think. Ever heard the phrase "She who talks first loses"?

CHAPTER 4

Be Your Own Best Host

TWO SIMPLE RULES APPLY to driving your party plan business.

Rule number one is to be your own best customer. Declare yourself a competitor-free zone. Use your products, give them as gifts, and display them in your home.

Rule number two is be your own best host. There is no better way to showcase your business than by hosting parties in your own home.

The first party will be your Launch Party (Grand Opening, Announcement, or Celebration). You have taken a giant step toward fulfilling the American dream of owning your own business. What better way to celebrate than with people who care about you?

Your Launch Party is a dress rehearsal and a chance to iron out the bumps in your presentation. But its foremost purpose is to showcase your business to friends and family and to ask them to support you by becoming your first hosts and customers.

Even if you have to borrow your sponsor's kit, the earlier you hold your Launch Party the better, so you can take advantage of the "Fast Start" rewards that every party plan corporation offers newcomers during their first months in the business.

A Successful Launch Party

The following steps will ensure your Launch Party gives your business the best possible start:

* Invite everyone. It's a celebration, and the more people who come to share the excitement, the better.

* Hold it in your home. If that's not possible, ask a close friend to host it for you or find a local venue. Your church, library, or community center may be willing to accommodate you, as may a child-care center after hours. Even a park could be fun.

* Make sure your sponsor is the first person you invite. Not only will you benefit from her experience, but her presence will show your friends that you are part of a supportive network.

* Be creative with your invitations. Use festive graphics and colored paper, mail them in envelopes stuffed with confetti, roll them into a cylinder, or send them in a balloon with instructions to inflate and pop the balloon to retrieve the invitation.

* Don't be so creative that you forget important details, such as when, where, and what time to arrive, plus an RSVP so you know how many to plan for.

* Promise lots of fun, food, and freebies to increase acceptances.

* If a friend can't come, say, "I'll miss you but I under-

stand. Would you like your own exclusive preview? I would love your feedback." Or say, "I have gifts to give my first ten hosts and I would love you to have one. Would you like to host a small party for your friends? You receive some amazing rewards for being a host, and wait till you see the products."

* Create a celebratory atmosphere with balloons or streamers but don't make your Launch Party so elaborate that you give the impression that the business is hard work. A few festive touches such as tying bows around the stems of glasses, serving drinks in glasses topped with strawberries, or dipping the rim of glasses in colored salt or sugar will convey a celebratory theme without going over the top.

* Ask a friend to help with refreshments so that you can focus on being a wonderful host. There is no point in being in the kitchen when you should be sharing your excitement about your new business.

* If you have many friends, hold more than one Launch Party. If you offer a choice of dates, friends are more likely to be available on one of them.

Start the party by thanking your friends for sharing this special occasion with you: "This is an exciting day for me and I can't think of a better way to start my business than to share it with friends."

Give them a taste of what their party will be like by keeping the talking part down and the socializing part up. Briefly introduce the products, the host rewards, and the business opportunity and then invite everyone to relax, have fun, and experience your products.

Make it easy for guests who wish to place orders by having

order forms ready, and ask them to let you know if they are interested in joining you. Have plenty of party and business bags ready.

Time your Launch Party for no more than two hours and close by inviting everyone to host a party for you. Have your calendar ready to take bookings. An "act now" incentive will start the ball rolling so I suggest you wrap several gifts and say, "These gifts are for my very first hosts, as my way of saying thank you for helping me get started. Of course you will still receive all the amazing host rewards. Let me show you."

Send your guests home with a host rewards brochure whether they booked or not. That will give you a reason to call and say, "Thanks for being there for me. What did you think? Did you take a peek at the host rewards?"

Set the high standard you will follow throughout your business by sending thank-you notes to everyone who attended, and immediately start coaching your new hosts.

Your Launch Party will be the first of many wonderful parties you host in your own home. Plan at least four self-hosted parties every year, and mix them up with different themes to keep them exciting. There's no better way to promote yourself than by being "the host with the most," and these parties will advertise, loud and clear, that you are in the party business.

To help you start, below are some example themes for your parties:

* An appreciation party for customers and hosts will build loyalty and generate more business.

* A mystery-host party will fill a vacant date in your calendar. Every guest goes in the draw to win the host rewards. If guests bring a friend, their names go in the draw twice.

* A party-crasher party is a fun way to encourage guests to bring friends you haven't met.

* The slower months of summer are the perfect time to host a pool party, a sunset soiree party, or a party with a beach, backyard, barbeque, or baseball theme.

* A celebration party is the ideal way to thank hosts and customers when you achieve a milestone. If you win a cruise, host a sail-away party to highlight the rewards that come with your business. Make sure you invite guests to join you on the next cruise: "If anyone is thinking they would like to do this, now's the time. The company just announced that the next cruise is to Alaska and qualification starts next month so anyone can achieve it. Who wants to share a cabin with me?"

* Invitations to "Join me for champagne, cake, gifts, and fun as you indulge in some retail therapy" will guarantee a good response to your "Beat the Winter Blues" or "Kids Are Back in School" parties.

* Invite moms with kids to drop by on the way home after dropping their children off at school to check out a new product range. If you don't want your home invaded by kids, ask the moms to stop by *before* they collect their children.

* Schedule parties to capitalize on the demand for celebration, themed, and gift products before Mother's Day, Father's Day, Valentine's Day, Easter, Cinco de Mayo, Fourth of July, Halloween, Kwanzaa, Diwali, Thanksgiving, Hanukkah, and Christmas.

* Invite friends and neighbors to an "Open Home" where they can come and go as they please. Black Friday is the perfect time to clear unwanted inventory before your customers empty their pocketbooks at the mall.

❋ Help last-minute shoppers with a cash-and-carry sale in the lead-up to Christmas. Entice them with promises of balloons and gifts for kids, hot apple cider for moms, and free gift-wrapping. If you expect a crowd, invite a college student to run your gift-wrap station in return for free products.

❋ Mini fund-raisers are a great way to build your network and show community spirit at the same time. In return for donating 10 to 15 percent of your sales to a local charity, you will reach a bigger audience.

❋ Invite your friends to party online. Add the chance to win big by offering every shopper a chance to win the host rewards.

❋ Schedule an annual "Bring Your Business Home" party to present the business to your most promising prospects. The launch of a new catalog, the introduction of a new range of products, or the start of a special incentive is time to say, "If there was ever a time to join the business, this is it."

 SUPERSTAR SECRET

The launch of your holiday catalog is the perfect time to invite customers to join as casual sellers in the weeks leading up to Christmas. Once they have had a taste of the profit they can make by helping friends and family do their holiday shopping, most of them will continue on in the new year.

You have to be organized to take advantage of opportunities. Schedule a Fast Start "How to Profit from the Holidays" workshop in advance so you are ready to train interested prospects immediately.

In addition to hosting parties, keep your parties fresh and exciting by learning from other party planners:

* ✽ Go to observation parties with your sponsor.
* ✽ Go to refresher parties with successful consultants.
* ✽ Invite your sponsor to your parties to give you feedback.
* ✽ Host your own "practice parties" to try a new format.
* ✽ Go to parties with other companies.
* ✽ Host parties for other companies.

The more willing you are to share your knowledge, skills, and experiences with other consultants, the more willing they will be to share theirs with you.

CHAPTER 5

Create a Bookings Bonanza

BOOKINGS ARE THE LIFEBLOOD of every party plan business. No bookings . . . no business . . . bye-bye goals!

If your goal is a new car that costs $15,000 and you earn $150 per party, you must do one hundred parties. If you consistently schedule ten parties a month, you will have your car in less than one year.

Even if you're working your business as a hobby, or combining it with a full-time job, you can manage ten parties a month, especially if you picture yourself driving those shiny new wheels. It all depends on how much you want it, and what you are prepared to do to get it.

If your goal is to unburden yourself of a $10,000 credit card debt and you earn $100 a party, you will need to schedule one hundred parties. Schedule one party a week, and it will take you less than two years. If you maintain a consistent schedule of two parties a week, it will take you just one year and save you thousands of dollars in interest payments and bank fees. Consistency is the name of the game. An erratic schedule of parties will produce erratic results.

Each party will have a ripple effect on your business. By doing two parties a week with an average of ten guests, you will interface with one thousand new people a year. Even a relatively low attendance average of five guests will produce five hundred new contacts a year.

New customers always spend the most, but it doesn't stop there. Many of them will become regular customers, some will become hosts, and others will join you in the business. A few could follow your lead to become your party plan superstars. When your superstars elevate to leadership roles, you will step up to higher levels of your compensation plan as long as you maintain a healthy personal business.

There's no downside to making bookings your number one priority. If you keep your calendar full, you'll always have a healthy business. The day you stop bringing in new customers is the day your business is in trouble. It may drift for a while but believe me your ship is slowly sinking.

Follow these eight steps to create the bookings you need to drive your business forward.

Step One: Organize a Separate Calendar for Your Business

Introducing a separate calendar for my business was one of the best decisions I made. I always knew how many bookings I had. My booking gaps leaped off the page at me and prompted me to pick up the phone.

If your calendar is crammed with commitments that have nothing to do with your business, you may think you're busy when you're not. Health and beauty appointments, household chores, and routine errands like taking the car in for maintenance or renewing your driver's license will fill your day if you let them.

If you want to live the life that most people only dream about, you have to set priorities, and that means scheduling personal commitments around your business. There's nothing like an empty page in your calendar to motivate you to lift your game.

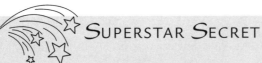

SUPERSTAR SECRET

Find a calendar that displays one month per page. With a separate business calendar you can check the status of your bookings at a glance and confirm bookings on the spot. You can hand it around at parties so hosts can select a date for their parties while you're busy with other guests. No prospective host should have to sort through the clutter of your personal commitments to find when you're available.

Take your calendar with you everywhere you go. There's no sense in leaving it in the car or at home when you're out and about.

Step Two: Plan Your Parties

Decide how many parties you will do and highlight the dates in your calendar. You will have to be flexible, but you can always find more dates or move a date if you have to.

Ten parties a month will build a strong foundation for your business. Even if you can't do ten parties a month, block ten dates to allow for postponements, cancellations, and dates you cannot book.

Note public holidays and school vacations to make prospective hosts aware of those dates. You don't want to make a booking only to have it fall through when the host discovers it clashes with a holiday.

SUPERSTAR SECRET

Aim to achieve every incentive your company offers. Work out how many parties you need to achieve them, add a few extras as a buffer zone, and mark up your calendar.

On average you can expect one in four hosts to cancel or postpone their parties. Don't take that risk. Ensure against disappointment by loading your calendar with parties at the start of the month. That gives you time to reschedule postponements later in the month, host your own impromptu party if a party is cancelled, or top up your sales with servicing calls when party sales fall short of expectations.

A Superstar's calendar looks like this:

Week one: Four dates highlighted for parties

Week two: Three dates highlighted for parties

Week three: Two dates highlighted for parties

Week four: One date highlighted for a party

Plan your party schedule that way and you will never have to say, "I missed a promotion because I had a last-minute cancellation," which in truth really means, "I missed a promotion because I left it until the last minute and had a cancellation when it was too late to make up the lost sales."

Step Three: Mark Dates That You Must Fill *Now!*

Use bright, shiny stickers to draw attention to dates that you are in danger of losing if you can't find a booking fast, or that best fit your lifestyle, such as the start of a new month or back-to-back parties on a Saturday when your partner can take care of the kids. Call them your star dates.

Shiny star stickers will leap off the page, and you can also theme your stickers to draw attention to Easter, Valentine's Day, Mother's Day, and Christmas bookings.

SUPERSTAR SECRET

Encourage potential hosts to book your star dates by offering them extra rewards. Although your costs will increase slightly, a little less profit is better than no profit at all. That's why movie tickets are cheaper in the afternoon, retailers schedule their sales at off-peak times, and restaurants offer early-bird specials. Bookings lead to more bookings, so it pays to invest a few dollars to attract them when you need them most.

Step Four: Keep Building Your Contacts List

You'll find it easier to make bookings with people who know and like you. That should be reason enough to service your customers regularly (and maintain close contact with friends, family, neighbors, and associates).

If your contacts list is too small for you to achieve your goals, use the "A to Z Memory Jogger" at the end of this chapter to conjure up more names.

Parties will always be your best source of contacts, but make it a habit to collect names, phone numbers, and e-mail addresses anywhere, anytime. Commit to adding to your list daily and contacts will pop up in the most unexpected places. Always be on the lookout and always have a pen and notebook handy to record details on the spot.

Step Five: Start Calling

Bookings won't materialize out of nowhere. You have to create them by talking to people every way you can: face-to-face, phone, text, e-mail, or online. Not everyone will say yes, so be prepared to make lots of calls. Your phone is your lifeline and the sooner you learn to love it, the sooner you'll grow.

Aim to be consistent and persistent. Schedule a daily "power hour" and call until your calendar is full. You can easily make ten calls in an hour if you stay focused. If you don't have time for a daily power hour, schedule as much time as possible. If ten calls yield one confirmed booking, it's an hour well spent.

SUPERSTAR SECRET

Don't let the clock determine your future. Commit to calling until your calendar is full and then call some more. When you're on a roll, think how good it will feel to say, "I'm booked solid this month, but I'd love to schedule you in as my first host next month."

It takes discipline to make ten calls day after day. But that's how you build your business. As a newcomer you can expect to interest one person out of ten. As you improve, so will your odds and you may find two out of ten are interested. When you hit your stride, three out of ten may say yes. Expecting more than that is unrealistic and will set you up for disappointment.

SUPERSTAR SECRET

Buy a set of ten shiny bangles. Every morning, place the bangles on your left wrist as a promise to yourself that you will make ten calls. Each time you make a call, transfer one bangle to your right wrist until you have transferred every bangle across.

The bangles will tell you how many calls you must make before you can call it a day. If you are in danger of allowing yourself to be distracted or discouraged, your bangles will remind you that you committed to making ten calls. They'll motivate you to find the time to squeeze in the extra calls instead of quitting before you reach your target.

> The bangles also make great conversation starters. When someone asks, "What's with the bangles?" you can say, "They make me $100,000 [or $50,000] a year!"
>
> If you know you won't have time to make ten calls, start the day with fewer bangles. Decide each morning how many calls you will make, but the rule is, once the bangles are on your wrist, you have to make the calls.

Monitor your calendar daily to ensure you're fully booked at least three weeks ahead, and have a backup plan for postponements.

 SUPERSTAR SECRET

Keep young children happy by bringing out special toys they can play with, or a favorite DVD they can watch, when mommy's on the phone.

Try to eliminate background noise when you're making calls. If you're distracted, it will come through the phone.

When you're enjoying family time, switch your phone to voice mail.

Step Six: Make Them an Offer They Can't Refuse

The more compelling your offer is, the more bookings you'll get. Always think, "What's in it for my prospect?" before you pick up the phone.

For example, "Hi Tayla. I'm wearing my party hat today. I've just received the spring catalog and it's our best ever. Would you like to be one of my first hosts for a spring party? I'm giving the first five hosts to book a special gift and I'd love you to have one."

Resist the urge to unleash an avalanche of information, and instead focus on what you can offer the person at the other end of the phone by saying, "I can't wait to show you our new catalog. It's our most stylish ever and the colors are a perfect match for your new family room."

Don't let excitement cross over the line into pressure. If you're not excited about what you're offering, you can't expect others to be, but fast-talk is not going to get you a booking. Pressure is a major turnoff, especially when you are calling prospects who like to think things through before they commit.

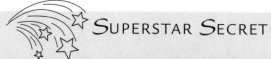

SUPERSTAR SECRET

Be more generous with compliments about your prospect than you are with praise for your products. For example, "You're such an amazing cook. I can't wait for you to taste test the new summer flavors."

Being new can be an advantage because you can say, "I'm really excited. I've just started my own business as a consultant for an amazing range of nutritional supplements. I need six parties to get started and I'm hoping you'll be one of my first hosts. The good news is you get lots of free products for helping me."

Don't be afraid to be yourself: "I'm excited but a little nervous, too. Can I practice on you? I have six gift vouchers to give away to my first six hosts and I wanted you to have one of them."

Step Seven: Spread the Word Wide

Seize every opportunity or excuse to attract bookings:

* Distribute product catalogs, samples, and host brochures to friends, family, and coworkers.

✻ Place a sign in your yard to let neighbors know how easy it can be to access their favorite products. Someone who has lost touch with her previous consultant will be thrilled to find you.

✻ Deck out your car with your brand logo and phone number. If you use magnetized banners and window clings, you can remove them when you want to.

✻ Send regular e-newsletters to your customers and contacts. An interesting subject line will encourage them to open it. Short, newsy articles will encourage them to read it. A compelling offer will encourage them to respond.

✻ Go viral to spread your message. The majority of Americans social network daily. Join in to win your share of business.

✻ Drive customers to your Web site by sending intriguing e-mail blasts with a live link straight to your offer.

✻ List your available dates on your online calendar with an incentive for any customer who "calls to book a party before I call you."

✻ Send postcards to announce new products, host promotions, or customer incentives. Postcards are easy to produce and inexpensive to mail, and you can guarantee they will be read—unlike a letter, which has to be opened.

 SUPERSTAR SECRET

Who could ignore this irresistible offer: "Book a party during your birthday month and get champagne and cake on me!"

Step Eight: Fish for Referrals

If you think of every person as a potential link to many more, you won't hesitate to ask for referrals. Do it by asking questions that will lead you to people who are the most likely to be interested in your products:

> To find your foodies, ask, "Who is the best cook you know?"

> To prospect shop for your spa business, ask, "Of all your friends, who takes the most care of their skin?"

> To find likely scrapbookers, ask, "Of everyone you know, who takes the best photos?"

When calling this last referred friend, say, "Hi Ella. Grace gave me your phone number. I met her at a scrapbooking workshop and she said you take the most beautiful photos. Did she say she'd given me your name? I love photography, too, and I'm a consultant with a scrapbooking company that sells only by party plan. We have a huge range of albums, accessories, and embellishments to scrapbook your favorite photos and we bring it all to your home. Would you like me to pop around and show you the latest looks?"

Be generous with rewards to those who give you referrals. A free product or a discount off a future purchase makes an inexpensive thank-you gift for an introduction.

 SUPERSTAR SECRET

Double the power of your rewards by offering them to the referring *and* the referred customer. The first reward will encourage your customers to give you referrals, and the second will encourage their friends to see you.

> Ask your referring customers to call their friends before you call them: "Expect a call from my friend Kelly. She sells those candles you admired at my dinner party. I gave her your name and she has a gift for you."

Calling can be a tedious chore or an exciting challenge. It's all in your mind, but if you don't have bookings, you don't have a business. If you're preoccupied with rejection, you're focusing on the wrong person.

SUPERSTAR SECRET

Don't allow yourself to be bruised by rejections. They come with the job. Instead, why not worry that someone you could have called, but didn't, bought, booked a party, or signed with someone else?

A to Z Memory Jogger

Your contacts list is a gold mine, and you'll be surprised at how many people you know when you start working on it with the following thought starters:

Accountant	Assistants
Acquaintances	Aunt
Active person	
Aesthetician	Babysitter
Anyone who uses my products	Bank officer
	Bar staff
Artist	Barista
Asks lots of questions	Baseball moms

Beautician

Best friends

Book club

Boss

Bus driver

Business owners

Busy person

Butcher

Cake decorator

Carpet cleaner

Cell phone contacts

Chamber of Commerce

Charity workers

Checkout operator

Checkout staff

Cheerleaders

Chiropractor

Christmas card lists

Church members

Classmates

Cleaner

Club members

Coach

College friends

Committee members

Computer support staff

Counselor

Country club members

Course participants

Cousins

Coworkers

Craft club

Dance club

Daughter

Daughter-in-law

Day care

Delivery person

Dental nurse

Dentist

Doctor

Dog walker

Drama club members

Drama coach

Dry cleaner

Electrician

Electrolysist

Elocution tutor

E-mail list

Empty nester

Engaged friend

Enthusiast

Everyone you meet

Ex-neighbors, associates,
  coworkers

Facebook friends

Fast-food workers

Father

Favorite person

First-home owner

Fitness coach

Flight attendant

Florist

Football moms

Former customers

Former direct seller

Former hosts

Former neighbors

Formerly in business

Friendly person

Friends

Friends' friends

Fun person

Fund-raising committee

Gardener

Girl Guide leader

Golf club

Grandparents

Grocer

Guest lists

Gym instructor

Gym members

Hairdresser

Happy person

Hard worker

Health club

Health coach

Herbalist

High school friends

Homeopath

Hosts

Hotel receptionist

House sitter

Housemaid

Husband's associates

Hygienist

Ice cream vendor

In debt

In-laws

Insurance agent

Internet services

Janitor

Journalist

Karaoke acquaintances

Kids' contacts

Kindergarten

Knows everyone

Landlady

Landscaper

Language teacher

Laser technician

Lawyer

Librarian

Life coach

Little League moms

Local retailer

Lollipop lady

Lost their job

Loves having fun

Loves life

Loves my products

Loves to shop

Loves to travel

Mail clerk

Mail delivery person

Maintenance crew

Manager

Manicurist

Massage therapist

Mechanic

Midwife

Mortgage broker

Mother

Mother-in-law

Music teacher

Nail technician

Naturopath

Neighbors

Nephews

New mom

Newlywed

Nieces

Night-class students

Night-class teacher

Nonprofit association
staff

No-shows at previous
parties

Nurses

Obstetrician

Old address books

Old school friends

Optician

Optimist

Other direct sellers

Over the back fence

Owns a business

Pageant contestants

Pageant organizer

Parents of kids' friends

Partners of coworkers and associates

Part-time worker

Party guests

Pediatric nurse

People I meet at the park

People who invite me to their parties

Performer

Personal trainer

Pet groomer

Pet minder

Pet walker

Pharmacist

Photo shop assistant

Photographer

Physiotherapist

Playgroup moms

Plumber

Pregnant

PTA committee

Qualities I admire

Queues or people I meet in line

Radiologist

Realtor

Receptionists

Relatives

Reporter

Retailers

Room service staff at convention hotel

Sales clerk

School staff

Server

Service clubs

Shopper

Siblings

Single parent

Sister

Sister-in-law

Soccer moms

Social circle

Social clubs

Sorority sisters

Spa technician

Sporting contacts

Starbucks

Stay-at-home moms

Students from high school, college, university

Successful person

Supermarket shelf
  stackers

Supervisor

Swim instructor

Tailor

Talented person

Teacher's aide

Teachers

Tennis coach

Therapist

Thrift store

Toastmasters

Tradesperson

Traveler

Twitter friends

Uncles

University classmates

Vacation friends and
  acquaintances

Vacation-home neighbors

Veterinarian

VIP customers

VIP hosts

Voice coach

Volunteers

Waitress

Walking-group members

Walks by my house

Waxing technician

Wedding guest list

Wedding planner

Weight-loss coach and
  support group
  members

Wives of my coworkers
  and associates

Wives of my husband's
  coworkers and
  associates

X-ray technician

Yoga classmates

Yoga instructor

Youthful person

Youth group leader

Zany person

Zoo worker

CHAPTER 6

Book Smart at Parties

THE BEST PLACE to fill your calendar is at parties. No matter how hard you have to work for them, the sooner you start generating bookings from bookings, the sooner you'll free yourself from the chore of cold calling.

Think Bookings

Commit to securing two confirmed bookings at each party. Every time you come away from a party without a booking, you sever the link between you and a plethora of potential customers, hosts, and business prospects.

Display Bookings

When guests arrive at the party, the first thing they will do is glance at your display. If all they see are products, they will get the message that you're there to sell. Period.

If you do what the average party planner does, you'll earn what the average party planner earns. If you want to earn the income party plan superstars earn, you have to do what they do.

 ## Superstar Secret

Would you prefer to take home a host pack or a party bag? I'd choose a party bag anytime.

Make your host literature pop by putting it into colorful gift bags. Top the bags with tissue paper. You can transport the tissue flat and fluff it out to decorate the top of the bags when you arrive at the party. Your party bags will attract attention and portray bookings in an exciting light.

Print cards that say "Free shopping spree" or "$XXX free products" (equate the value of the coupon to your average host gift) and clip these cards to the outside of each party bag with plastic pegs in vibrant colors.

Take a moment to picture your display with eye-catching party bags strategically positioned among your products. Put yourself in your guests' shoes and imagine what they will think:

"Are they gifts?"

"Are they free?"

"Will I get one?"

And the answers are:

"Yes!"

"Yes!"

"Yes!"

Your party bags will also remind you to ask for bookings. The number one reason you will fail to get bookings is because you do not ask for them. You allow yourself to run out of time, you lack the courage, or you indulge in negative self-talk: "No one looks interested." If you use party bags, you can't avoid talking about bookings because they are the centerpiece of your display.

Demonstrate the generous host rewards by giving your host an attractively wrapped gift at the start of the party and saying, "Before we start, I want to thank Nikki for inviting us into her home tonight. My hosts are the reason I have a business and that's why I love giving them gifts. Nikki, thank you for introducing me to your friends. This is one of our most popular products and I know you're going to love it."

Alternatively, you can hand your host a basket with an assortment of gifts and invite her to choose her own gift.

Without you having to explain further, guests will receive the message loud and clear that bookings mean gifts.

Talk Bookings

Excite prospective hosts with tantalizing descriptions of what's in it for them.

Point to your party bags and say, "Who loves to party? Everything you need to host your own party comes in this party bag, including how you can earn a shopping spree on me. I'll give you the details later, but if you like the idea of hosting a party for your friends, one of these bags has your name on it."

Pick up your calendar and say, "This is my party calendar. It has all my available dates highlighted. All you have to do is find a date that suits you and it's yours! And the best part is, if you book a party before I ask you to, you'll receive a special gift in addition to your shopping spree!" Hold up an attractively wrapped gift and hand your calendar to the nearest guest so it can be passed around. It will cost very little to start the bookings rolling if you stock up with gifts when they are on sale.

There is always a risk of cancellations when you give gifts straight up, but the risk is small when you compare it to what will happen if you have no bookings. If you prefer not to take that risk, carry gift tags with you so you can label the gift and say, "This is yours. I'll bring it to your party."

SUPERSTAR SECRET

Holding up the gift at the new host's party will create the perfect lead-in to a booking commercial: "You may be wondering why Kaydence is receiving two gifts. She earned this extra gift for being the first person to book a party at her friend Jan's party. If you think you would like a party, make sure you're the first to book a date so you get the special gift."

You're only a few minutes into your party and you've already presented four booking commercials:

* Thanking your host with a gift
* Talking about your party bags
* Showing your party calendar
* Tempting early-takers with an extra gift

SUPERSTAR SECRET

Keep your parties fresh by mixing up your presentations. One of my favorite ways to attract bookings is to pop a selection of reward coupons into sealed envelopes and place them inside the party bags. These coupons could include:

* $10 cash to spend at your party
* 10 percent off your order today
* Choose any gift from my basket

> Clip your star dates (i.e., best available dates) to the out-side of the bags. Draw attention to the dates and explain that the first guest to take the date wins the mystery reward inside the envelope.

Guests will have different reasons for booking, so remember to highlight different benefits each time:

* Free gifts will appeal to bargain hunters and the cash-strapped.

* Customers who are building a collection will appreciate a chance to add more items.

* The convenience of shopping without leaving home will suit busy moms and working girls alike.

* Party girls will love the idea of socializing and shopping at the same time.

* Other guests will see a party as a welcome change from a night in front of the television.

The shorter your booking commercials are, the more effective they will be, so practice until you can present them in fifteen seconds, for example:

"Who can think of friends you keep meaning to call but you never seem to get around to it? Hosting a party is a great way to catch up with friends and earn free gifts at the same time."

"Who thinks it's fun to shop in Brooke's living room? Why schlep around the mall when we bring everything to you?"

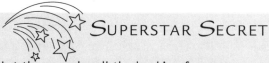

SUPERSTAR SECRET

Let the rewards sell the booking for you.

"Wait until you hear about our host program. First, you receive a free gift just for booking. Second, you get to choose 10 percent of your party total in free products. Third, you get exclusive half-price specials that only hosts can order. This month, it's these gorgeous stackable bowls. They are perfect for picnics and I've had hosts who booked just to get them. But that's not all. For every guest who books at your party, you get one half-price product of your choice.

That's four fabulous reasons why you should book your own party. Who's already feeling tempted to host a party?"

Focus on the reasons why now is a good time to book:

"Next month is our anniversary month so it's when we have our best host rewards. If you're thinking about hosting your own party, next month is definitely the best time to do it. Why not earn as many free products as you can?"

Talk about your most popular products:

"I have had more people book a party to get this collection at half price than anything else."

SUPERSTAR SECRET

A fun way to showcase the generous host rewards is to pick an extroverted guest and invite her to role-play with you by asking, "Will you be my hypothetical host?"

Hand her each gift as you outline your host program, starting with the thank-you gift, the rewards she will receive for sales, then bookings, and any bonus rewards. Your hypothetical

> host will soon have an impressive amount of free products in her
> hands. At the end, say, "Don't you wish you could take all this
> home with you now? See how quickly your rewards can add up?"

Pampering your host is a surefire way to attract bookings. If you sell spa products, treat her to a hand, foot, or face massage so her guests will want a taste of the VIP treatment, too. Ask her, "How does it feel?"

She will no doubt reply, "Wonderful," and you can ask guests, "When was the last time someone pampered you? Who is thinking, right now, 'I wish I could take Phoebe's place'? One of the perks of being a host is the luxury of your own beauty treatment. Your skin will glow for days."

Or say, "Whose feet were tingling when Phoebe had her foot massage? Perhaps they're telling you to book a party so they can be pampered, too!"

Encourage interaction. The more that guests interact with you, the more easily you'll spot your best prospects for bookings. Get them to interact by asking the following questions:

"Who has hosted a party before?"

"Who with?"

"How was it?"

 SUPERSTAR SECRET

You will add to your credibility if you can say, "Isn't it fun having parties? This is my job and yet I still book parties for other consultants. I love having my friends over and I love getting free products."

Make sure you vary your parties. If they're all the same, you won't inspire future hosts. You can expect to see familiar faces at parties, so keep renewing and refreshing your parties to keep the excitement alive:

* Theme parties are a great way to excite hosts to book and book again. Try Yummy Mommy, Bridal, Bachelorette, Birthday Bash, New Baby, Housewarming, Summer Barbecue, Glitz-and-Glamour, Spring Bling, or Pajamas-and-Tiaras parties.

  "Who has a friend who is getting married? Bachelorette parties are great fun."

  "Who has a friend with a birthday coming up? My spa shows are a perfect way to pamper the birthday girl and her friends."

* If everyone is captivated by a popular television show, suggest a preshow party. Finish the party before the show starts or suggest that the host record and play it after the party.

* If you sell food, wine, or kitchenware, suggest a gourmet party for couples so husbands don't miss out on the fun.

* Schedule alfresco parties on the patio throughout summer.

* Suggest "shared host" parties where one host opens her home and the other brings refreshments. Both hosts invite their friends and share the host gift equally.

* Offer a staff-room party during lunch breaks or after work:

  "Does anyone here work with a lot of people? We can bring the party to your work. It's a fun way to break up [or end] the day."

✻   Offer catalog parties to working girls. Give them a stack
    of catalogs, a bunch of order forms, and perhaps a few
    samples to show friends and coworkers for one week. At
    the end of the week, total their sales and offer them the
    same host rewards as your regular hosts.

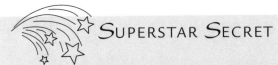

SUPERSTAR SECRET

Tempt busy hosts with a restaurant party. Most restaurants have
separate seating areas for private events and the host won't have
to do anything except invite her friends and show up.

If bookings are slow in coming, start the ball rolling by saying, "The first person who books a party can choose any gift
from my basket." Once you have broken the ice, more bookings
tend to follow.

Always do a group invitation toward the end of your presentation. If you've been distracted by more extroverted guests,
someone with a less outgoing personality could fly under your
radar: "If you have had fun tonight, think about hosting your
own party. This is your last chance to book a show before I ask
you, and get a bonus gift."

If you are marking your best dates with stars, say, "Thanks
Pearl and Sarah for booking a party. I can't wait. I think I have
one star date still available, so if you think you can bring a few
friends together at short notice, why not take it and earn the free
gift? Impromptu parties are often the most fun and you can take
your party bag home with you tonight."

Don't become an order taker during one-on-one time. Show
an interest in what guests are ordering, not how much they
spend, and watch for signals that it's time to ask for a booking.

If someone is trying to choose between several items, pick

the most expensive and say, "Why don't you get the most expensive one free by hosting your own party?"

Or say one of the following:

"Did you know you could get over $100 in free products if you invited a few friends over? It'll be fun and you look like someone who has lots of friends."

"I love your enthusiasm. You would make an amazing host. Why not have a party?"

"Have you thought about having a party? You have so much on your wish list, you may as well get some of it free."

"I'm excited you like the products. Why don't you book your own party? All you have to do is invite a few friends over and I'll do the rest."

"You have almost the whole collection and it would be a shame not to complete it. How about having a party so you can get the rest free?"

Pick the person you would most like to be a host and say, "I would love to do a show for you."

 SUPERSTAR SECRET

Don't trust your judgment. Learn to ask the person who you feel is least likely to host a show. You can't know who will say yes unless you ask. Only by training yourself to ask everyone with the same air of expectant optimism will you get the bookings you need to achieve your goals.

If a host has one booking at the end of her party and you're struggling to get the second so that she can achieve her two-booking credit, offer a "double up" incentive. Promise guests who book that you will add their order from this party to their party total when you calculate their host rewards.

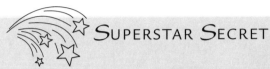

SUPERSTAR SECRET

Suggest that the host secure her booking credit by booking a second party for friends who couldn't make this one.

If she says, "All my friends are here," you can ask, "Do you think everyone bought everything they wanted? Did you? If you book another party, you will all be able to buy the products you didn't get tonight, and in five weeks I'll have the new fall collection to show. You can be one of my first fall hosts."

Never forget that your best booking tool is a great party. The more fun guests are having, the more likely it is they will host their own party. The more fun your host is having, the sooner she'll book a repeat performance. People book parties for fun, friends, and freebies. Make sure your party is a stunning showcase of all three.

CHAPTER 7

Sponsor to Succeed

THE MOST REWARDING INVESTMENT you can make in your business is in your sponsoring skills. No matter how much you earn, selling is a job. The moment you stop selling, your income will stop. Sponsoring makes it a business.

Here's your mantra:

"Sales are my income for today. Bookings are my income for tomorrow. Sponsoring will be my income forever."

Most party planners say the number one reason they started a business is . . . someone asked them. It was not a premeditated decision. They happened to meet the right person at the right time and they signed up. Your job is to make sure that right person is you.

If you ask people without a party plan business to identify what the sticking point was, the overwhelming majority will say,

"There's no reason. I never thought about it. No one has ever asked me."

The number one reason people don't start a party plan business is not because they're too scared, busy, lazy, young, or old or they don't think they can sell. It's not because they're happy with the job they have, or they're too timid to switch. It's because no one approached them.

The magic word in sponsoring is "ask." Not everyone is going to be interested. You ask everyone because you don't know who will or won't be interested. Don't try to be a mind reader or second-guess your prospects. Starting, or not starting, is their decision to make. Your job is to extend the invitation to as many people as possible, and in the best way possible.

Don't let inexperience stop you from sponsoring. Enthusiasm and excitement will always count more than experience, and you and your new recruit can learn and grow together. Start sponsoring from day one.

Don't let distance hold you back. Technology has removed every obstacle to sponsoring long distance. From signing to mentoring your new consultant, everything can be done by phone, Skype, and the Internet. Long-distance team members can log on to Webinars and attend meetings by Web cam. Make an effort to visit your team members in person if possible, but if it's not practical, you can meet up twice a year at National Convention and the annual incentive trip. What special times those will be!

 SUPERSTAR SECRET

Commit to attending National Convention and the annual incentive trip every year. Mark them on your calendar as soon as dates are released and be sure to register early. If you set aside a few dollars from every party for registration, travel, and accommodation expenses, you will hardly notice the cost. If you intend to fully earn your way, you will still need cash for miscellaneous expenses, so a travel fund is always a good idea.

If you keep a log of your activities, most of your costs will be tax deductible.

The greatest barrier to sponsoring is not that there aren't enough prospects, people aren't interested, times are tough, or any other excuse you care to use. The greatest barrier you have to overcome is hesitation.

Learning to sponsor takes both patience and persistence. But you've already learned that from your selling experience. Can you remember the guest who raved about every product you demonstrated but then slipped away without ordering a single item? Remember the one who gave you nothing but blank looks throughout your sales presentation but then surprised you with a huge order?

You can't predict what will happen, but the more people you talk to, the greater your odds of success will be. Every party planner has driven across town for a host who promised ten guests but delivered only two. Another time, when expectations were at rock bottom, the planner has hit the jackpot with a record-breaking party.

It's the same with sponsoring. It's a numbers game. You have to be prepared to ask many people in order to hear the word "yes."

If only it were as easy as yes or no. Some prospects may come close to signing but then get cold feet or sign with another company. Some will sign up with an abundance of enthusiasm that fades after they place a few orders. Some will sign up and do nothing, and others will do a lot. A few will succeed beyond your wildest imagination. That's what makes the business interesting and the rewards spectacular for the few who achieve party plan superstardom.

Nothing will stop you from reaching your goal if you've already factored in the faders and falterers. The only way you will fail is by doing nothing or by clinging to bad sponsoring habits when they're not working for you. The sooner you ditch your bad habits, the sooner you'll see results.

Bad Habit #1: Focusing on Yourself

Sponsoring is not about you; it's about your prospects. Their needs, interests, experiences, circumstances, and priorities will be different from yours and different from those of the prospect you talked with yesterday.

It's harder than it sounds to put your own feelings aside. Even I still sometimes have to remind myself of this. I grew up in a poor home, so financial security is something I am deeply passionate about. But I am sometimes guilty of overemphasizing *my* goals.

At a recent National Convention I ran a workshop on how to set meaningful goals, and I used debt as an example. When I asked members of the audience to share their goals, one volunteered, "I want to pay off my credit cards."

But I could see in her eyes that there was no passion behind her words, so I asked, "Are you sure?" There were a few seconds of silence before she smiled and said, "I don't really care about debt. I just want to shop!"

Her true goal was a closet full of shoes, and as the words came out of her mouth, her eyes lit up like a Christmas tree.

A few minutes later, when I asked another what her goal was she said, "I'm with the shoe lady!"

It's not your role to work out what your prospects want.

That's their job. Your job is to find out *what* they want and show them how they can have it.

Bad Habit #2: Talking About Your Company

It's easy to talk about how long your company has been in business, the charismatic founders, and how much the plan pays out at each level, but those details belong in the *Guinness Book of Nobody Cares*. Think how irritated you would be if you couldn't buy a sandwich or a skirt without being harangued about the origins of the business.

If there's a time for a talk about your company's history, founders, manufacturing standards, or home offices, it's at training—after your prospect has signed. Prospecting is the time to connect with people and for them to connect with you.

Bad Habit #3: Being Predatory

Sponsoring is not a manhunt. If you act like a predator, your prospects will act like prey. Showing scant regard for their circumstances and feelings may produce some short-term success but you won't make it far because prospects will race for the nearest exit when they see you coming—just as you would if someone tried to ambush you.

Bad Habit #4: Words!

Repeat after me: "Words are not my friend." When your lips are working, you're learning nothing. The more time you spend talking, the less time your prospects will spend listening.

Sponsoring is not about finding the right words; it's about finding the right people.

Bad Habit #5: Thinking Prospects Are Doing You a Favor by Joining Your Team

The exact opposite is true. Aren't you grateful to your sponsor for introducing you to the business? What if your sponsor had hesitated out of indifference or fear of rejection? If you love what you do, you'll be excited about paying it forward.

Bad Habit #6: Seeing Sponsoring in Black-and-White Terms

A "no" may have been closer to a "yes" than you think. Very few of our decisions are black and white. Mostly, they fall into the gray zone. We weigh up the pros and cons before deciding one way or another.

What can tip the scales from a "yes" to a "maybe" or a "no" isn't that your prospects are not sold on your business but that they are not sold on you. I've met thousands of successful party planners who said no to one person and yes to another. It was how they were approached that made the difference.

Bad Habit #7: Thinking That Your Business Is Right for Everyone

Sponsoring is a process of matchmaking. The reason you talk to as many people as possible is to find a match. When there's no match, it's not a big deal. But what if there were a match and you held back? What if you denied people the chance to take control of their life because you got stage fright or passed them by? What if you were so focused on your products that you left no time to talk about the business?

To become a sponsoring superstar, you must banish your bad habits and replace them with good habits.

Good Habit #1: Opening Many Doors to Your Business

The more doors you open to your business, the more people will come in. A party plan business can benefit so many different people on so many diverse levels. You will grow faster by targeting a wide range of prospects.

Moms should be right at the top of your prospect-shopping list. The U-turn from a "live to work" to a "work to live" culture has opened up a whole new world of opportunity for you to build a team. A party plan business empowers moms to stay true to their family-first values and meet their fun, friendship, and financial needs all at the same time.

Think of people who are spending the best years of their children's lives at the office. How different would their lives, and their children's lives, be if they used their talents to start a business from home? The difference between being a working mom and a mom who works is putting family first.

Look for full-time moms. Any party plan mom will tell you that spending time in adult company is one of the things she values most about her business.

Seek out working women who are stuck in the wrong job. However well paid they are, no one will spend their retirement years wishing they had spent more time at work.

Career women are great prospects. The more ambitious they are, the more they should question the wisdom of allowing someone else to decide what they're worth. Who wouldn't want to write their own paycheck, even if it means working harder?

Seek out business owners who may be fed up with working long hours only to see the bulk of their hard-won profits siphoned off by the landlord and the bank.

Look for workers who are facing voluntary or involuntary retirement. The prospect of not working can be scary for those who have neither money nor plans for their time. A party plan business will put them in the driver's seat. They can choose when to start and when to stop working—and when you love what you do, it doesn't feel like work.

That you can start a party plan business while still working a full-time job widens your scope of prospective team members. Think of people who:

*   Want to start a new career without the time and expense involved in retraining.

*   Are seeking variety from a job that offers little stimulation or satisfaction.

*   Need stopgap income between jobs.

*   Are looking for a way to make up for lost income when an employer has cut back on overtime hours.

*   Are concerned about having enough to get by if they lose their job. In an uncertain economy, everyone needs a six-month emergency fund.

*   Want to take advantage of the tax breaks that come with running a business from home.

Many successful party plan superstars say they started out intending to stay for only a short time before discovering that party plan was the career they had been seeking all along but they just didn't know it. That's why you have to open your doors wide.

Don't overlook people who have been in the business before. Turnover happens in all lines of work and many direct sellers experience one or two different companies before they find the perfect fit.

Integrity dictates that you should never approach consultants who are active with another company. Once they leave all bets are off. There are millions of former party planners who may be excited at a second chance to shine.

When you meet them, try to be specific about what is new, exciting, and different about your business:

"The training is incredible. I have learned so much."

"The products are different from anything you will see in stores."

"The company pays for the host rewards so I keep more of my earnings."

You have an advantage if you have been in the business before, as you can be specific:

"I used to feel guilty because I never found enough time to service my customers. My new company sends a monthly newsletter direct to my customers, with my name on it. My customers think it comes directly from me. I love seeing orders come through even when I'm not actively working."

Think of yourself as a talent scout on the lookout for people who can benefit from a party plan business. You never know when and where you'll spot them.

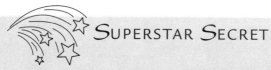 SUPERSTAR SECRET

Recruiting will always be easier when you know who's most likely to be interested. Find out who your best prospects are from my book *Be a Recruiting Superstar*. It's available from most retail and online booksellers or my Web site, www.marychristensen.com. For pricing on bulk copies, see the front of this book for details on how to contact the publisher directly.

Good Habit #2: Exposing the Gap Between What People Have and What They Want

It's not what we have that motivates us to make changes in our lives; it's the gap between what we have and what we want.

For many of us that gap is cash. You'll meet people who need money to pay bills, and others who want to start a retirement fund.

Look for people who have a gap between their income and their dreams. They may have enough money for day-to-day expenses, but they want to travel, upgrade their house, own a vacation home, drive a better car, or send their kids to the best schools.

Whenever there's an income gap, we have two choices: Either give something up or earn more money. I know which option I choose. Life is far too short to accept a hand-me-down, settle-for-less lifestyle.

Your prospects' gap may not be money. It could be education, status, recognition, personal growth, social, or any other reason people start a party plan business. Everyone has a different gap. Your challenge is to expose it and excite your prospects about filling it with a party plan business.

Good Habit #3: Asking Thought-Provoking Questions

It's far more important to be interested than it is to be interesting. The more questions you ask, the better your conversations will be and the sooner you will discover your prospects' perspectives and priorities. You will make more prospects interested in the business by being interested in them than you will by trying to get them interested in you.

Superstar Secret

The secret to becoming a great communicator is to ensure that the other person is enjoying the conversation as much as you are. When you encourage people to talk about their interests, opinions, perspectives, and experiences, they will open up to you.

Ask boring questions and you'll get boring answers. Ask open-ended questions, and you'll encourage people to ramble. Ask highly focused questions, and you'll discover what really matters in their life.

Try asking these questions to reveal a need for your business opportunity:

* "If you could change one thing about your job, what is the first thing you would do?"

* "If you discovered $1,000 in your wallet right now, what would you buy with it?"

* "How different would your life be if you paid off your debts?"

* "If you were given a $100-a-week pay raise, what would you do with it?"

* "If you won two first-class air tickets to fly anywhere in the world, where would you go? And whom would you take with you?"

* "If you could give your family one special gift right now, what would it be?"

* "If you could make just one personal dream come true, which dream would you choose?"

By having prospects answer these questions, you will see

how they focus their thoughts and reveal their innermost feelings. Try the questions on your friends and family to discover what matters most in their lives before you try them on your prospects.

Good Habit #4: Showing Pride in Your Business

When someone asks you about your job, you have the perfect opportunity to promote your business:

* "I have a great job. I sell fragrant candles at home parties."
* "I'm a party planner. I demonstrate and sell inspirational wall expressions."
* "I am an independent consultant for a leading brand of spa products."
* "I have my own business selling the most amazing educational books."

Create a story that people will enjoy hearing and relate to on a personal level. Leave out the irrelevant or uninteresting details so that your story is exciting and inspiring, as in these examples:

"I'm a teacher, but I always dreamed of going on a safari in Africa. I knew I was never going to save enough from my job, so I started a small, part-time business selling natural beeswax candles. Working for myself is more satisfying than I ever imagined it would be, and I have saved nearly half of the money for my trip."

"Last year my mom had a health crisis and it was a huge wake-up call for me. I decided to start taking better care of myself. A neighbor had recommended that Mom try an amazing nutritional supplement and I started taking it, too. It made such a difference to both of us that I decided to sell it. The supplement changed my health, and the business has changed my life."

"I'm a mom. I have two beautiful daughters and I love spending time with them. But I don't want to give up my independence. So I do two parties a week to meet people and enjoy a little 'me time.' But best of all, the money I make pays for all the extras we couldn't afford before."

Good Habit #5: Sharing Your Business at Every Opportunity

Keep listening up for reasons why your prospect will benefit from your business:

* To someone who seems unsettled at work: "Have you ever thought about going out on your own? I'm building a small business from home. It has opened up a whole new world for me."

* To someone with debt or cash flow problems: "Ever thought about starting a part-time business to bring in some extra cash? The extra income I make from my business has made a huge difference."

* To a friend or close relative: "Ever thought about us working together? Think of the fun we could have."

* To a neighbor who has similar products on her kitchen counter: "Did you know you can buy these wholesale?"

* To friends, family, neighbors, or coworkers who talk about gaining weight: "Try one of my low-calorie snack bars. They're only eighty calories and they're delicious."

Good Habit #6: Keeping Your Message Simple

Don't complicate matters by telling your prospects more than they need to know. Timing is everything. A volley of information too soon will more likely alienate prospects than get them excited. Take it gently.

The purpose of your first approach is to get them interested. They are more likely to agree to a next step (i.e., meet with you or invite you to send more information) if they are intrigued by what you say. Overexplaining takes away the reason for you to follow up.

Most budding party planners start out with small goals. Many times those small goals blossom into big goals once they have had a taste of the business. No one wants to commit to something she doesn't fully understand, and if you make it sound like a big deal, most prospects will be frightened away. Talk instead about "earnings per party," and use soft-sell phrases such as "small business" and "part-time."

Stay clear of jargon. Don't use industry-speak, such as "upline," "downline," "width," "depth," and the abbreviations IBO, PV, and BV, or you will confuse or annoy your prospects.

Good Habit #7: Following Up

Never leave prospects in limbo. Always have a "next step" in place. If prospects say yes, sign them up straight away. The sooner they sign, the sooner they can start realizing their goals.

If they are on the fence about signing up, keep the communication lines open with the following:

 *   Invite them to an upcoming event.

* Give them a book, CD, or DVD that will help them learn more about the business.

* Send them a magazine that features your company, referring them specifically to articles that match their circumstances and tell them: "You should check out the article on page 46. It's about one of our top people and she reminds me of you. She was a career mom, too."

* Invite them to listen to a call that outlines the business. It's not my favorite technique (I find it impersonal) but it can't do any harm if the person conducting the call is charismatic. Make sure you join the call so you can follow up with the question "What part did you find the most interesting?"

 Superstar Secret

Never give the impression you are trying to force a decision, or that you are more eager than your prospects for them to sign.

A great way to keep them interested but not pressured is to use a little reverse psychology by saying, "Now that you know what it's about, put the idea to the back of your mind for a few days. If you find yourself thinking about it, maybe we should talk some more."

Always treat your prospects with integrity. If they say no, send a handwritten note thanking them for taking the time to meet with you. If you make them feel embarrassed about their decision, they won't want to hear from you again.

The principle behind sponsoring is simple: You are looking for people who are perfect for your business because your business is perfect for them. Just as the princess had to kiss a lot of frogs to find her prince, you have to sift through a lot of people to find your party plan superstars.

CHAPTER 8

Coach the Most from Your Host

You and your host form a fantastic partnership. You win if she wins! She wins if you win!

So don't sit back and relax once you have the booking. The more excited, confident, and organized you are, the more excited, confident, and organized your host will be.

Create a separate folder for each party to keep everything together from the time the booking is confirmed until you have completed your follow-up calls. A simple checklist on the front of the folder will make it easy to check that each step is completed.

Prepare your party bags in bulk so you have at least ten ready to go. Take four to every party, and carry two with you, so you're ready to seize a booking opportunity anywhere, anytime. Include in your bag:

❑ A host rewards brochure

- ❑ A current host incentive brochure
- ❑ A "shopping spree" wish list
- ❑ Product catalogs
- ❑ Order forms
- ❑ A guest list that includes spaces for twenty-five guest names and contact details, the date it must be returned to you, and your contact details
- ❑ A business opportunity brochure (unless you prefer to send it later, as I recommend)
- ❑ A collection envelope showing your full contact details.
- ❑ A "Host Challenge" card (see Figure 1 on page 163 in Chapter 15, "It Pays to Play")
- ❑ Twenty-five invitation postcards

Carry a supply of blank thank-you cards with you. When you get a booking, write a note thanking your new host and confirming the date of her party, and drop it into her party bag.

SUPERSTAR SECRET

Personalize invitations by placing small stickers in different colors or designs on the front right-hand corner of each one before you give them to your host to send out. Place duplicate stickers in an envelope for your guest attendance draw. You can buy sheets of stickers from most craft stores.

Draw attention to the sticker when you call guests two days before the party by saying, "Take a look at your invitation and you'll find a sticker on the front right corner. It's your ticket into my lucky guest draw, so bring it with you as you have to be there to collect."

This simple step alone will decrease no-shows, because most people will find it hard to resist a chance to win a free gift.

Coaching Step-by-Step

Each of your hosts will be different. How you coach each one will depend on your relationship, her confidence, and her experience in hosting parties. You will also have to take into account the amount of time you have to coach your host between the booking and the party.

The three keys to a great party are:

1. Guests!
2. Guests!
3. Guests!

Ten guests is a good target, but why stop there? If your brilliant coaching results in an average of one extra guest for each party, your business will increase by 10 percent. Imagine if the extra guest became your next superstar.

The main reason hosts fail to deliver enough guests is poor host coaching, so plan to make five coaching calls if possible. The first call will take around fifteen to twenty minutes, and the others will take no more than five to ten minutes. An hour spent on coaching your host is a tiny investment when you consider the potential of every party. Coaching also creates a perfect opportunity to bond with your host and to begin the process of turning her into your next consultant.

Schedule Your First Coaching Session as Soon as Possible

Coaching is as much about the feel-good factor as it is about the details, so be as enthusiastic as you are focused. You don't want your host to feel stressed, uncertain, or nervous. You want her to feel confident, excited, and motivated to make her party a success.

The following steps will give your host the best chance of a successful party.

Express Your Appreciation and Confidence in Her as a Host

An appreciation call goes a long way in boosting your host's confidence:

> "Thanks for booking a party with me. I can't wait to meet your friends and I know your party is going to be a huge success."

Ask Questions That Will Tell You What She Expects for Her Party

"What do you love most about our products?"

"What do you think your friends will enjoy most?"

"What did you enjoy most about Ella's party?"

"What was the main reason you booked? Was it our amazing host rewards?"

There are many reasons she may have booked:

* For the host rewards.
* It seemed like a fun way to gather her friends together.
* She wanted the pampering and attention.
* She was caught up in the moment and booked on impulse.
* Her friends were all having parties and she felt it was her turn.
* She wanted to help her friend get the booking credit.

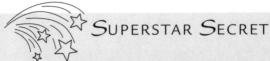

SUPERSTAR SECRET

If your host felt pressured, she may be regretting her decision. Win her over by saying, "I can't thank you enough for booking a party. Am I right in thinking that you are doing this to help Stacey? That makes you pretty special so I'm going to do everything I can to make you happy you did."

You Can Safely Assume Rewards Will Be One of the Most Important Reasons a Host Books

Talk about the rewards up front by saying, "We're a team! My job is for you to earn as many free products as possible. Your job is to fill the room." You want your host to focus on attendance, so try not to distract her with anything else.

Explain what your best reward level is, for example, $500 sales with two bookings, and encourage her to aim for that level or higher by saying, "Let's go for as many free products as possible."

Helping your host create her wish list is the fun part of host coaching so work through the catalog with her. By making suggestions and being excited about her choices you will build a closer partnership. Suggest that she maximize her rewards by selecting lower-price items for her free products and higher-price items for her half-price items.

Make her wish list your goal for the party and help her understand how to reach it by sharing information about your parties:

> For example, "My average is $500 but I want you to have a better-than-average party. The best way to make that happen is to invite lots of guests," or,

> "My average sale is $50 per guest, so ten guests will help us reach your $500 target. If you can get twelve guests, all the better."

If she booked from a friend's party, be more specific:

"Jenny had eight guests and her sales were $400. Let's aim for ten guests and $500 sales; $500 is magic because you get an extra half-price item at that level and I know you have your eye on [name a product]."

Help Her Create the Guest List

Explain that she will need to invite twenty-five guests in order to get ten. The more suggestions you make the more people she will think to invite. Most party plan companies suggest FRANK: friends, relatives, acquaintances, neighbors, and people she knows through her kids. You can expand FRANK by asking questions that will prompt her to think of more names:

"Who do you know who has the best parties?"

"Who do you know who has the most parties?"

"Who has invited you to a party?"

These should be the first guests she invites, as there is a good chance they will book their own party and help her achieve her half-price host credits.

Suggest guests who regularly use your products. They are more likely to place high orders: "Who do you know who wears the most jewelry [is a fabulous cook, always has a camera with her, loves going to spas]?"

Suggest guests who will liven up the party:

"Of all your friends, who is the most fun?"

"Who has the most friends?"

"Who gets the most excited by new things?"

Suggest that she extend an open invitation to coworkers, church members, Facebook friends, and the moms at day care.

If you run out of ideas before you run out of spaces on her guest list, use my "A to Z Memory Jogger" (at the end of Chapter 5) to help her think of more people.

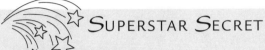

SUPERSTAR SECRET

Encourage your host to fill her guest list from the bottom up as she thinks of whom she would like to invite. If she has spaces for twenty-five names, suggest that she write her first potential guest in the twenty-fifth space and then add each new name upward until she lists number one.

If your host works from the top down she might be tempted to stop when she thinks she has run out of names. Gaps at the top of her guest list will stand out. By working upward she is more likely to keep adding names to reach the top.

The Sooner Your Host Starts Inviting Her Friends, the Better

Remind her that the longer she delays, the more likely it is that her guests will have made prior commitments.

SUPERSTAR SECRET

Recommend that your host call her friends to invite them personally before she sends the invitations. Everyone wants to feel special, and if she says, "It will be even more fun if you're there," she will increase acceptances.

If your host says, "I don't have time to call everyone personally," tell her, "I understand. The reason I recommend you call everyone first is that people are more likely to come if they are personally invited. It makes them feel special. Plus, it's hard to generate the same enthusiasm in a postcard or e-mail. I want this to be a huge success for you, so if you find time to make the calls, I promise it will be worth it."

Coach your host on how to sell the party to her guests. Stress that her goal is to tempt guests to come, not to explain everything in detail. Here are some suggestions that you can share with her:

> "I'm having a party next Thursday and I've invited a consultant from a gourmet food company to come and demonstrate some fabulous summer recipes. Can you make it?"

> "It's time we all got together and I thought it would be fun to have a scrapbooking party."

> "I'm having a girls-night-in spa party next Wednesday and you are at the top of my list of people I hope will come."

> "I'm having a lingerie party and I'm inviting only ten guests. I really want you to be one of them."

If your host has been to a party, encourage her to share her experiences when she calls:

> "I just went to a handbag party and had so much fun that I booked my own party. They were the most fabulous designs. Are you free on the 16th? I really want you to see them."

> "I had the best time at Nikki's party and learned some fabulous new decorating ideas. And they were so simple. I can't wait for you to see her fabulous wall designs."

> "We're going to have a great time. My skin was glowing for days after Maria's spa night. I booked a party so I could do it all over again."

> "Wait until you see the jewelry. The designs are gorgeous. I would have bought almost everything if I could have afforded to."

> "I'm having a few friends around next Thursday for a home-makeover party. I have a linen consultant coming to show us

the spring collection. I remember you saying that you were thinking about redecorating your guest room."

"I have just discovered the most fantastic product. Did you know that you can publish your own memory book? I'm going to start one for each of my children, and I've invited someone to come and show us how to do it. Helen and Jenny are coming. Do you want to come?"

Set Your Host a Guest Target

"Host Challenge" (see Figure 1 on page 163) is a fun way to focus your host on what she needs to do to get the best results. Review each of the squares with her, asking, "Do you think you can do that?" Make sure you ask if she has any questions and explain that if she achieves twelve or more guests she can check both the "ten-plus guests in attendance" and the "twelve-plus guests in attendance" squares.

If you prefer a simpler challenge, add these words to her guest list: "Eight is great, nine divine, ten sensational!" to focus her on a ten-guest target.

If you prefer not to offer a challenge, say, "If I receive your guest list by Friday, I have a small gift for you." The guest list is precious because it will help you make your own reminder calls, follow up with guests who didn't come, and add names to your database. In my experience, if there's no guest list, there's no party.

Suggest She Carry Extra Invitations and Product Catalogs in Her Bag to Take to Work, Playgroup, Etc.

Remind her to tell those who can't make the party to place an order and encourage her to aim for at least two pre-party orders by saying, "Outside orders count toward your party total and will get you off to a great start."

Agree on the Date She Will Mail the Invitations (After She Has Called Her Friends)

The more buzz she creates, the more people will want to come. Recommend that she send a follow-up e-mail or text a few days after the invitations are sent. Help her set up e-vites through your Web site so guests can RSVP online and you can both track how many guests are coming. A timely reminder call may encourage guests to commit.

Address Her Questions and Concerns Up Front

Hosts who book impulsively often question their decision the next day. No host wants her party to be a flop and some people are natural worriers. When you know what she's thinking, you can deal with it.

Here are some ways to manage her concerns about her party:

> **Concern:** "I don't think I can get as many people as Linda did."
>
> **Answer:** "This is your party and we're not comparing it to anyone else's. I really appreciate your booking and I know Linda did, too, as your booking earned her an extra half-price item. Invite as many guests as you feel comfortable inviting. I am happy doing small and large parties and I want you to enjoy your party."

> **Concern:** "My house wouldn't hold twenty-five people!"
>
> **Answer:** "I agree. Not many houses can hold that many. The reason I suggest twenty-five is that not everyone will be able to come, and some guests will say they're coming but not make it on the day—their kids get sick, their husband is delayed at work, or they can't find a babysitter. All my hosts say they had to invite twenty-five to get ten guests."

Concern: "I'm not doing this for the rewards."

Answer: "That's great! Most hosts are motivated by the rewards. But I want you to have them. You deserve them and it's my way of showing you how much I appreciate you. So let's go for them anyway."

Concern: "I don't care how many people come. I just want my friends to have fun."

Answer: "I agree. We want this to be fun for everyone, including you. I find that the more guests who come, the more fun the party is. Have you ever been to a party where there weren't many people? The atmosphere is not the same. When there are lots of guests, everyone relaxes and has a great time."

The important thing is to make your hosts feel confident and excited that their party will be a success. Some hosts love calling their friends, sending out invitations, and preparing refreshments. Others are happy to mail the invites, post their party on Facebook, and buy a few snacks at the supermarket. By asking them questions, listening to their responses, and observing their actions, you can adapt your coaching to each host's interests and expertise.

Make Sure You Ask Her to Keep Her Refreshments Simple

Keep refreshments simple for these three reasons:

1. You want her to enjoy her party.

2. Elaborate refreshments send the message that hosting a party is expensive and time consuming, which will dissuade those with limited funds or limited time from booking.

3. Food can be a big distraction.

Gently encourage your host to request that no children attend, and if that's not possible, to arrange a babysitter or provide a DVD and snacks in another room.

Set a date and time for the next call and end on a high note by saying, "I think we're going to make a great partnership. You take care of filling the room and I'll work on turning your wish list into your very own free shopping spree."

Schedule Your Second Coaching Call About Ten Days Before the Party

A lot may have happened since your first call and your enthusiasm will come at the right time.

Start by checking that she has completed these steps:

* Sent you her completed guest list
* Called everyone on her guest list
* Mailed the invitations

Her feedback will determine what to cover in your second call. Compliment her on what she has achieved and remind her what needs to be done, such as sending you her guest list or mailing her invitations.

Hosts who haven't sent their invitations will usually promise to send them right away, but some will make an excuse, such as "I have been so busy."

If you sense that your host is genuinely pressured, say, "The last thing I want is to make this stressful for you. It's supposed to be fun. Why don't I mail out the invitations? All you have to do is prepare the guest list. We can even set it up so guests can RSVP online. I can bring a plate of cookies, too, if that helps. No one expects elaborate snacks."

Ask how many guests have RSVP'd and what the response has been (the industry average is 65 percent, so she will probably have some chasing up to do).

If she's had a few "Sorry, I can't make it" responses, reassure her that there is plenty of time to invite more people and then make more helpful suggestions:

"Has anyone recently moved into the street? Why don't you invite them?"

Suggest she say, "Hi, I'm Kelly. I live at number 19 and I've been meaning to pop over and say welcome. Are you settling in okay? Here's my name and phone number in case you need help with anything. I came over because some friends are coming to my house next Tuesday for a jewelry party and thought it would be a perfect chance for you to meet some neighbors. I know they'd love to meet you."

The more suggestions you offer, the more likely it is your host will think of people she has forgotten.

For neighbors she hasn't seen in a while she can say, "It feels like we never have a chance to say hi, so I'm hosting a party next Thursday. It's very casual. A friend sells the most awesome handbags and she's bringing them but it's really just an excuse to get together. I'd love it if you could make it."

Here's a suggested call to a neglected friend: "I haven't seen you for ages so I'm having a party on the 15th to get my friends together before school breaks for the summer. I've asked some-one who sells leisurewear to bring her summer range along so we can see the latest styles."

Suggest she say to family members: "Are you free on Saturday? I have some friends I'd like you to meet and I have organized a chocolate specialist to come and give us a demon-stration on how to create delicious desserts with chocolate."

To her child's teacher, she could say: "A lot of us have kids in your class and we thought it would be fun to get to know you a little better outside of school. We're making it a spa party, which should be fun."

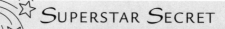

> ## 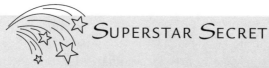 SUPERSTAR SECRET
>
> Remind your host that an invitation is a compliment. No one wants to feel left out or forgotten. All of us would prefer to have the chance to say no than to be forgotten or excluded from the guest list.

The easiest way your host can increase her guest count is to invite her guests to bring a friend. This works well in dicey weather and if guests are driving long distances because an arrangement to carpool makes it harder to cancel. Suggest that she say, "Hi Maria. I'm looking forward to seeing you at my party. It's going to be fun, so bring a friend. There's plenty of room."

> ## SUPERSTAR SECRET
>
> It will sound even better if your host names the friend: "Hi India. Can't wait to see you next week. I wondered if you wanted to bring your sister Briar along, too. She's fun and it would be great to see her again."
>
> Think how flattered Briar will feel when India calls and says, "Emma's having a party next week and she asked me to call and invite you along, too."

Coach your host never to say, "You don't have to buy anything." If a friend is reluctant, or asks if she will be expected to place an order, your host can say:

> "Of course not. There is no pressure at all. My problem was the opposite. I wanted everything."
>
> "I have invited the consultant I met at Jan's party, and she put no pressure on anyone at all. We had a great time."

Encourage your host to take a proactive approach to her party. After she has sent her invitations, suggest that she call her friends to ask if they have received their invitation and if they are coming.

Remind your host to show the catalog to guests who decline the invite, and to invite them to place an order. Highlighting a couple of great specials will help encourage outside orders. Remind her to collect any payments, including tax and shipping, so that the order can be added to her party total.

 SUPERSTAR SECRET

Don't expect your host to remember every detail. Make it easy for her by highlighting key lines on the order form so that she can see exactly where to add any applicable charges, such as tax and shipping, to outside orders.

If you have a universally popular or exceptional product or offer, it may pay to leave samples for your host to show.

Answer any questions your host may have, and say, "There are only ten days until your party. Are you excited?" before confirming a time for your next call.

Schedule the Third Call About Four Days Before Her Party

Now it's crunch time! You want your host to feel excited and encouraged but now is the time for her to pull out all the stops to produce the numbers.

Check how many confirmed guests she has and congratulate her on the total by saying, "You're doing great!"

Remind her of the rewards she will get from a great turnout and come up with some more suggestions if necessary.

SUPERSTAR SECRET

Keep a list of suggestions by your phone so you can recall them easily:

"Can you think of someone you haven't seen in a while, perhaps a former work colleague or neighbor?"

"Is there anyone from church you would like to get to know better?"

"Is there someone from another department at work?"

"Did you say your son plays baseball? Why don't you invite the baseball moms?"

"Did you post your party on your Facebook page? It's not too late."

"What about your Twitter friends?"

Remind her to call guests two days before her party to make sure they are coming.

If she says, "I don't have time to do the reminder calls," tell her, "I understand. The reason I recommend that you make reminder calls is that some people who say they're coming, later forget. I can't begin to tell you how many times I've heard guests say, 'Just as well you reminded me. I had completely forgotten.' If you can find the time to make a few calls, it will make a huge difference. You'll reach most people on their voice mail anyway so it shouldn't take long."

Ask once again, "Have you met anyone or thought of anyone else you would like to have come? Anyone you forgot? Why not call them now? Better late than never."

There will be times when hosts try to postpone or cancel their party. Some cancellations are inevitable and happen for valid reasons, such as a child's illness. But some hosts try to postpone or cancel when they hit a snag, such as:

* They're struggling to get numbers and they are panicking.
* They've lost heart after a few "I can't make it" RSVPs.
* Guests who were coming have pulled out.

This can be disheartening and your host may feel that her easiest option is to cancel. Don't make it so easy for her. You have already invested a lot of time in this party, so do everything you can to make it happen. Here's what you can say:

"Don't worry. I saved that date for you and, to be honest, it's too late for me to get another booking, so let's go ahead anyway. Some of my best parties have been small, but let's see if we can think of some people you have forgotten."

Or:

"I'm sorry your friends can't come but I won't get another booking at this stage, so if we can make this work, I would really appreciate it. It's not too late to think of some friends you may have forgotten to invite."

"Remember the fun we had at Kim's party? Yours is going to be great too, whoever comes."

Stay positive and focused on the fun. Chances are that all she needs is reassurance. It's a fact of life that some guests will have prior commitments and that some won't want to come. Some people may feel that they'll be pressured into buying, or they're struggling financially and they want to stay away from temptation.

You don't want reluctant guests at your party, but a disappointing response is usually because your host hasn't made her party sound exciting. Coaching her on the right words to say will help build attendance:

"Instead of going to the spa, I'm bringing the spa home so we can really relax."

"There'll be a cooking demonstration and then we get to sample everything. Yum."

"I met the consultant at another party and she's a lot of fun. Everyone had a great time."

"Make sure you don't miss out. There are going to be a few surprises."

End this coaching call by saying to your host, "I am really looking forward to this. You're doing a great job." Then set the time for your final call.

Preventing cancellations is better than having to formulate last-minute rescue plans. Date your parties as soon as possible. The shorter the time between the booking and the party, the more likely the date will hold. The farther out parties are scheduled, the higher your risk of a cancellation or postponement.

 SUPERSTAR SECRET

If your backup plan fails and you find yourself with an empty date in your calendar, don't take it as a license to stay home, watch *The Biggest Loser,* and eat brownies. You allocated the time to your business, so use it to start connecting.

With a little ingenuity, you can always find someone to talk to: the salesperson at your favorite store, the server at your local restaurant, your Realtor, or the person working out alongside you at the gym. Are you wondering how you can start a conversation cold? Get people talking about themselves and they'll soon be asking *you* questions.

If you are staying home, shut the door, put your booking bangles on your wrist, and pick up the phone.

Schedule the Fourth Call Two Days Before Her Party

Start by saying, "We're almost there! I'm excited for you!"

Hopefully, her party is progressing full steam ahead but if she says, "I have had a few cancellations," you can say, "Don't worry. Smaller numbers mean I can spend more time with each guest. But why don't you call everyone and ask them to bring a friend? Perhaps a sister or a neighbor they can carpool with? I love party crashers, so I'll bring gifts for anyone who brings a friend who wasn't on our original guest list."

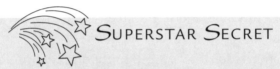 SUPERSTAR SECRET

Don't rely on your host. Make your own reminder calls as well. It takes only a few minutes to call each guest and say, "Hi Cayce. It's Jan, your consultant for Ellen's party on Thursday, and I'm calling to say thanks for coming. I'm looking forward to meeting you and it's going to be fun. Don't forget to bring your invitation to be in the drawing to win a special gift."

Some guests have every intention of coming to the party, but when they get home from work and put their feet up, they think, "Do I really want to go out again?" Your friendly call and reminder that their invitation is a ticket in your lucky draw makes it more likely they will make an effort to attend.

Make Your Fifth and Final Pre-Party Call on the Afternoon of the Party

Call your host and say, "It's Samantha calling. I just wanted to remind you that I'll arrive around 6:30 p.m. to set up our party."

Check that you have the right directions to her home. Remind her to serve refreshments at the end of her party, so guests will not be distracted, and to serve them in the party room so guests will not wander off. Ask her if she has any questions and wish her good luck.

You have done everything you can to make the party a success for you and your host, and it's time to turn it into a booking, sponsoring, and sales bonanza.

Seven Keys to a Productive Host-Coaching Program

1. Coaching is not about one successful party. It's about building long-term relationships. Try to do your first coaching session in your host's home so that you build rapport faster. Continue your coaching calls by phone. E-mail is a great way to update and exchange information but it won't excite, inspire, and enthuse your host.

2. Keep the focus on numbers. What you focus on, your host will focus on. Remind her to overinvite because declines, last-minute opt-outs, and no-shows are a fact of life.

3. Contact is the key. Encourage your host to call guests three times:

    *   First call: Before she sends out the invitations, she should say, "I really want you to come so I thought I would call first to let you know. But I'll send the invitation as well so you have everything in writing."

* Second call: After invitations have gone out, she should call again to say, "I'm checking to make sure you received your invitation. Can you come?"
* Third call: Twenty-four to forty-eight hours before the party, she should call to say, "Looking forward to seeing you. We're going to have fun." A friendly reminder call will reduce no-shows.

4. Always get the completed guest list from your host. It's a gold mine of contacts, including guests who don't make the party.

5. Don't get caught up in details or create the impression that it's work for you or your host. Parties are all about having fun.

6. Think "host-for-life." You won't have a shortage of repeat and referring hosts if you consistently deliver great parties and you build a mutually rewarding relationship with your hosts.

7. Think of every host as a potential consultant, regardless of her current level of interest. If and when their circumstances change, you don't want to be caught napping.

Sample Letters

These sample letters will make it easier to correspond with your host. While you must cover important details, such as how to post her party online and how to deposit funds, your correspondence should always be upbeat.

Following is a letter to confirm the booking:

Hi Beki,

Thanks for hosting a party with me. I am excited about working with you to make your party a huge success!
The details I have are:

Date: August 25
Start time: 7 p.m.
Finish time: 8:30 p.m.
Address: 5 Princeton Street, Oakville, CA 98765
Phone: 321-678-543X
E-mail: beki@partyplansuperstar.com
Your guest target is: Ten!

The more guests who attend, the more free products you will earn, so invite at least twenty-five guests to allow for those who can't come and those who don't make it on the day.
I'll see [or call] you on Thursday morning at 10 a.m. to share some tips for making your party a success. If you have any questions, feel free to call me anytime before then.
I am excited to meet your friends and have a great time with you all.

Samantha Walker
[insert your contact details]

Following is a letter to thank your host after the party:

Dear Beki,

    Your party was awesome! Thank you for being such a wonderful host.

    Your sales were $[XXX] so your free shopping spree total came to $[XXX].

    Because Paige and Trinity both booked a party, you earned two half-price items in addition to your free shopping spree. Well done!

    Your final delivery details are [XXX XXX].

    Your final payment details are [XXX XXX].

    I know your friends will be thrilled with their products and I hope you will book another party with me soon. Meanwhile, welcome to my VIP Host Club. I'll keep you posted about exciting invitations and offers coming your way.

With thanks,
    Samantha
    [insert your contact details]

PART THREE

Let's Get the Party Started!

CHAPTER 9

Set the Stage

GREAT PARTIES DON'T HAPPEN BY LUCK or accident. You have to make them happen and my best advice is this: Think big!

Set clear goals for every party. If you think sales, you'll get sales. If you think sales and bookings, you'll get sales and bookings. If you bet on all three—sales, bookings, and recruits—you have a good chance of hitting the trifecta.

Take a snapshot of your perfect party. Mine looks like this:

* Ten guests
* $500 in sales
* Two bookings
* One new recruit

Think "10–5–2–1" and imagine how your business will thrive when you meet those targets. Of course, some parties will meet your expectations, some will exceed them, and some will fall below them. Highs and lows happen in any business. But one thing is certain: The higher your aim, the higher your results will be.

Assemble your party supplies in advance so you can set up quickly at the party. If you have visited your host's home during coaching, you will know the space you have to work with and the challenges you have to work around.

The better your tools, the easier your job will be. The tools I include in my party tool kit are simple and inexpensive and will dramatically increase your chances of reaching your sales, booking, and sponsoring targets:

* A calendar with your available dates highlighted to make it easy for your hosts to find a date that suits you both, and sparkly stickers marking the dates you want to tempt hosts to book.

* Two pens for each guest, in contrasting colors to make it easy for them to mark the products they want now while noting their "maybe" or "next time" choices. The contrasting colors will help you spot whose wish list is bigger than their budget. You can suggest to those guests that they host their own party.

* Duplicate stickers for the invitations you have personalized, or tickets for your guest draw.

* Instructions and supplies for games you will play to identify your best booking and business leads.

* A selection of attractively wrapped products for gifts and prizes, placed in a basket and tucked away until you need them.

* Three festive party bags. Not only will they stand out at the party, the festive presentation makes it less likely

that hosts will take them home and forget about them. The longer that hosts delay calling their friends, the more likely it is someone they were counting on to come will have made other plans.

✻ Three large gift bags topped with tissue for your business literature. The larger size will send a visual message that the business is a bigger prize than the booking and will remind you to talk about the business throughout your presentation.

✻ Name tags for each guest, so you can remember and use their names.

✻ An order form for each guest, with special items or recommendations highlighted so guests can easily locate them.

✻ Guest slips, which are a gold mine of information about each guest. You can print four per page and still include all the information you need:

Name:

Cell phone:

Landline:

Best time to call (morning/afternoon/evening/weekend):

E-mail:

My birthday is:

I am interested in (check as many as you like):

❑ New products

❑ Specials and promotions

❑ Joining your VIP Customer Club

❑ Hosting a party

❑   A personal consultation

❑   Organizing a fund-raiser

❑   Receiving your free newsletter

❑   Finding out more about the business

❋   A watch that will remind you to start and finish on time.
    Not only is it a basic courtesy, every minute you go over
    will cost you money and goodwill. If guests are thinking
    more about the time than what you're saying, or they
    rush off before placing an order, you lose. If the party
    starts late, cut something out rather than go overtime.
    It's better to leave guests wanting more than less.

❋   Your prospect-shopping list. They're not your only
    prospects but they're your best ones, so keep an eye out
    for them. You can find out who your best prospects are
    in my book *Be a Recruiting Superstar*, but your list
    should include:

❑   Moms

❑   Teachers

❑   Cheerleaders

❑   Performers

❑   Artists

❑   Nurses

❑   Former direct sellers

❑   People who need money

❑   People who are dissatisfied with their job

❑   People who are using/wearing products similar to
    yours.

❑   Realtors

- ❏ Business owners
- ❏ People with big dreams

 SUPERSTAR SECRET

Name tags will double as selling tools if you invite guests to share information about themselves beneath their name:

* If you sell cookware, ask guests to write their favorite (or least-favorite) food as a fun talking point.

* If you sell books, games, or toys, ask guests to write the first name and age of their children on their name tag so you can see who has children at the appropriate age for your products.

* If you sell beauty products, ask guests to write one personal-care item they couldn't live without so you can hand them a similar product to test.

* If you sell candles or fragrances, ask guests to write their favorite scent so you can include it in your presentation.

The easiest way to identify hot prospects is to ask direct questions:

"Do we have any teachers here?"

"Who has kids?"

 SUPERSTAR SECRET

Transport to your parties as little weight and bulk as possible. Pack your tools, products, and paperwork into a roll-on tote (or two) and arrive at your parties looking professional and organized.

The first thing guests will do when they arrive is look at your display, so think of ways to get maximum effect—the wow factor—for minimum effort.

*   Cover the table with a light-colored cloth with a soft sheen that will flatter your products. Use black cloth if you want to create a more dramatic effect.

*   Landscape your display at different heights and angles by placing the boxes the products came in, or weightless polystyrene blocks, under your cloth.

*   Your products are your draw card but your goal is to generate bookings and business leads, so position your business and party bags first and then display your products around them.

*   Give bestselling products prominent positions at opposite ends of the table so guests are not tempted to cluster in one area.

*   Arrange matching products in collections.

*   Draw attention to new, favorite, or overlooked items by placing a small "My pick of the month" or "New item" card alongside them.

*   If you wish to display your Starter Kit, set it out on a separate table. An easier option is to display laminated photos of the kit.

*   Theme your display for Mother's Day, Father's Day, Valentine's Day, Easter, Cinco de Mayo, Fourth of July, Halloween, Kwanzaa, Diwali, Thanksgiving, Hanukkah, Christmas, Spring, Summer, Winter, and Fall but don't overdo the accessorizing. Keep the focus strictly on your products, bookings, and business.

*   Employ lighting to enhance your display. Soft lighting

will showcase the flickering light of candles, candlelight will add ambience to spa products, and spotlights will make jewelry sparkle. If you keep a portable light and extension lead in your car, you can bring it in if you need to. Halogen bulbs are best because they emit a clear white light.

As a rule of thumb, less is more. Give your products space to breathe. I've been to parties where products are overflowing off the table, stacked on the floor, and perched on every available surface. I can tell you this: Clutter creates confusion. Give guests too many choices and they may end up choosing nothing.

Think of the way upscale stores artfully display a few select pieces to convey a message of exclusivity. Compare that to the clutter of a junk store and you'll get the picture.

If you need mirrors, keep them handy to encourage guests to stay close by. If guests wander off in search of a mirror, you will lose the group dynamics that give parties their magic. Here's a tip: Mirrors without a frame won't compete with your products for attention.

The more senses you awaken, the better the ambience you will create:

* Play appropriate music to create a festive mood at holiday parties.
* Arouse taste buds with the aroma of baking cookies at gourmet parties.
* Waft soothing candle scents to relax guests at spa parties.

Don't have everything out on show. Surprises are a great way

 ☆ SUPERSTAR SECRET

If your products permit, treat guests to a sensory experience as they walk in the door: a dot of moisturizing hand cream to massage into their hands, a light spray of fragrance on the wrist, a delicious morsel of food to taste test.

Highlight the product you have sampled on the order form and remember to refer to it during your presentation.

You can even turn it into an opportunity to spot a hot prospect:

"Who can guess the fragrance of the hand cream you sampled as you arrived?"

"Who can name the spice in the sample I gave you when you arrived?"

When guests respond with correct answers, compliment them and remember to refer back to their talent when you ask them to join:

"You have a great sense of smell."

"You have sophisticated taste buds."

to attract attention, so keep a few items hidden and reveal them at the right time: new products, great specials, or bonus gifts that will encourage guests to increase their order. Then you can say:

"Oops! I almost forgot. If you spend $80 today, you will receive this set of holiday candles absolutely free! But only while stocks last."

Always keep in mind that your most visible display is . . .

you! Make sure you are a walking, talking billboard for your business. Never use or wear outdated products, no matter how much you love them. The only time it's okay to say "It's one of my favorites but we no longer have it" is *never*!

Prepare to Party

On the day of your party, leave nothing to chance. Ask your host for directions and program your GPS or print a route map to the house. I learned not to take directions for granted. One-way streets, road closures, obscured street signs, resident-only parking—I've encountered them all and usually when I least expected an eventful journey.

Load your car at least two hours before your planned departure time in case you have to deal with a last-minute family issue or phone call.

 SUPERSTAR SECRET

If you have children, including them in your preparations is a great way to teach them that it's a family business.

One of my favorite consultants has a Disney credit card that she holds up and says, "Mommy's off to make money for our Disney vacation." Her kids fall over themselves helping her load the car.

Another one calls her party nights "Daddy's night." Special meals, games, stories, and privileges are strictly reserved for Daddy's night!

With a little effort, you can make anything special if you plan ahead. When your family is happy, you will feel happier about leaving them.

Whether you work inside or outside the home, leave your day job behind so you can concentrate on your business. Think of the drive to the party as time to transform yourself into the relaxed, confident, and successful businesswoman you are.

The next two hours are full of wonderful possibilities. You are about to meet your next consultant, two new hosts, and a new group of lifetime customers. You could be about to meet your next team leader, manager, or director.

Revisit your goals over and over until they are embedded into your brain: "One new recruit, two bookings, and $500 in sales . . . One new recruit, two bookings, and $500 in sales."

Enjoy the silence, lift your mood with upbeat music, listen to a motivational audio, or rehearse your presentation—whatever it takes to transport yourself physically and mentally to your dream job—introducing your products and business to a roomful of new prospects.

Aim to arrive thirty minutes before the party but don't surprise your host before she's ready. An early knock on the door will upset any host's equilibrium. No matter what pressures you've had, whether unexpected delays at home or traffic hassles en route, take a deep breath and enter her home as though you haven't a care in the world.

No doubt your host has had her share of challenges. Sending the conversation up a dark alley sets the wrong tone for the party, which should be a welcome break from planet reality. If you need an outlet for the drama, save it for your blog. Your demeanor, voice, and actions must demonstrate that you have the best job in the world.

Set up quickly. You won't inspire your host to become your next consultant if you create the impression that your display requires an advanced degree in design. Remember to ask permission before you move objects or furniture and don't forget to set lighting and music that will embrace guests as they enter your party.

Pre-Party Host Coaching

Remember to spend time with your host before guests arrive. Her wish list is your goal for your party. If you're working smart, you'll bring the products she has chosen with you so that she feels halfway to owning them already.

But don't be shy about recommending other products. Her wish list is just that. Invite her to select items she likes from your display. Once her guests arrive, she will be busy playing host and may not have the time.

Ask her guests questions so you can identify your best prospects:

* "Have you been to any parties recently. Who was the host?"
* "Is there anyone else you think is likely to host a party?"
* "Who do you think would make the best host? Why did you think of her?"
* "Who's the most social of all your friends?"
* "Of all your friends, who do you think would make the best consultant? What made you suggest her?"
* "Do you know anyone who is looking for work?"
* "Have any of your friends been direct sellers like me?"

Once the first guests arrive, you must concentrate on making them feel welcome, but make sure you continue to give your host extra attention throughout her party. She deserves to feel special, and you are showing her friends how they will be treated when they book a party.

CHAPTER 10

Make Your Parties Sparkle

GUESTS HAVE GIVEN YOU THEIR TIME, but everything else you will have to earn. Deliver a mediocre party and you can expect mediocre results. If you want spectacular results, you have to deliver a spectacular party.

What makes a party spectacular? It's SPARKLE!

"S" for Socialize

Socializing and shopping make the perfect cocktail. Whether it's a girls-night-in spa experience, a scrapbooking workshop for moms, or a wine-tasting soiree for couples, parties are social events first.

Don't set yourself apart or be in a rush to start your presentation. Think, "How would I like my consultant to act if I were the host?" and you will know exactly what to do. When you are comfortable in your host's home, everyone will be more relaxed.

We do business with people we know and like. Give guests an opportunity to know and like you. Even the slickest presentation will fall flat if you don't connect on a personal level.

"P" for Play

Don't be a control freak. Encourage participation and interaction. Play games. Ask interesting questions and encourage feedback. Go easy on the information and focus on making your party a fun break from a routine or stressful day.

"A" for Action

Guests will make a conscious decision to:

* Buy your products
* Book a party
* Join your team
* Some of the above
* All of the above
* None of the above

Your job is to spark their desire to place orders, book parties, and join your team. If you're not achieving the results you want—change your game plan.

"R" for Relationships

Build relationships to build your business. Do everything you can to build the bonds that will lead to repeat orders, bookings, referrals, and recruits:

* Spend quality time with each guest.

* Take an interest in their lives.

* Show them courtesy and respect.

* Make them feel special.

* Follow up, follow up, follow up.

"K" for Kindness

Make your party a highlight of their day:

* Be generous with gifts and prizes.

* Express appreciation for large and small orders alike.

* Go out of your way to be helpful. Keep a few popular items in your car, so if a guest wants something right away, you can say, "You're in luck. I have one with me." If you don't have it with you, say, "I can drop it off [or ship it] tomorrow."

* Find ways to compliment your host:

  "Your home radiates warmth."

  "I've really enjoyed getting to know you."

  "Your party is by far my best this month."

  "I'm impressed by how organized you are."

  "Thank you for pulling out all the stops to make your target of ten guests."

"L" for Learning

Unless guests are learning something new, you shouldn't be talking. Approach your parties from new and exciting angles to keep them fresh and interesting.

Your parties must always be duplicable so your team members can follow your lead, but it takes a little extra effort to blend the information in your company manual with tidbits you find on the Internet and in magazines so that you can give them extra punch.

"E" for Entertainment

Parties are showtime. You may have a captive audience but it takes an entertaining performance to keep them captivated.

 SUPERSTAR SECRET

My business was beauty, and I quickly learned that the way to make my guests book parties and buy my products was to tap into their fascination with themselves.

THE SEVEN SINS OF SKIN CARE
By highlighting the seven key causes of aging, I prompted many guests to start a serious skin care program and my sales benefited.

DO YOU HAVE A MODEL FACE?
By showing my guests how to measure and compare their bone structure to the so-called perfect face I escalated my contouring and shaping products from slow movers to top sellers.

COMPLEMENT OR CLASH?
I loved showing guests how to choose colors that flattered their natural skin tone. Once they saw the difference a shade could make, they were eager to order a whole new palette of colors.

BEAUTY PERSONALITY

By helping guests identify their beauty personality (my categories were sporty, spicy, trendy, romantic, natural, earthy, funky, glamour, and chic) I sparked their interest in a total makeover and all new products—mine!

Leaving my guests wanting more helped me secure the next booking. By focusing on only one topic at each party and promising a different one to the next guest who booked, I generated my future bookings.

At one party, I met the features editor for a local paper and she wrote a story about my parties. That led to exposure in a national newspaper, which led to an invitation to write an advice column, and later to take the reins as beauty editor of a national women's magazine. The exposure was a major turning point for me.

Small ideas can lead to big breaks in your business. If you can stand up and speak in front of your peers, you can do anything. The only way you can guarantee that nothing will happen is to do nothing to stand out from the crowd.

Guests deserve more than a presenter on autopilot. Let your personality shine through your words and actions. Sprinkle your presentation with humor, share interesting stories and anecdotes, and encourage guests to do the same. If guests seem restless, inattentive, or distracted, you're probably boring them and that will destroy your chance of inspiring them to buy, book, and join the business.

When your parties SPARKLE, your sales, bookings, and business leads will skyrocket.

CHAPTER 11

Step into the Spotlight

PARTIES ARE PAYDAYS, but you will have to work hard and smart to hit the jackpot.

Sales are your instant profit, bookings your future profit, and recruits could be your lifetime profit! Keep all three top of your mind from the moment the first guest arrives until the last one leaves.

It's not enough to think business, bookings, and sales, or display business, bookings, and sales. You have to give significant talk time to all three.

If you allow sales to dominate your parties, you will never build your business beyond the most basic reward level. You have to weave all three components throughout your party. If you're as interested as you are interesting, people will listen.

Let the party and business bags act as reminders of your goals and measures of your progress. At the end of the party, all six of them should be in the hands of your best host and business prospects.

Every party gives you four chances to work your magic:

1. Meet-and-greet time
2. Presentation time
3. Closing time
4. One-on-one time

I'll cover the first two in this chapter. In Chapter 12, you'll learn how to close, and in Chapter 13 you'll learn to make the most of your one-on-one time.

Meet-and-Greet Time

Allow at least fifteen minutes to get to know your guests and for them to get to know you. Introduce yourself as they arrive and thank them for coming. Help with their name tag, pens, and paperwork, and invite them to browse your display. Then relax and enjoy their company.

Start identifying your best prospects immediately. Who's the bright light? Who's the most interested? Who's the most interesting? Who has children? Who's wearing your products? Who's on your prospect-shopping list?

Asking questions will help you get to know them:

"How do you know Ellen?"

"What made you decide to come tonight?"

"Do you have children?"

"Have you been to any other parties recently?"

If you start your presentation too early, you'll be talking to strangers and you'll deny guests time to mix, mingle, and peek at your display. Meet-and-greet time also allows latecomers to slip in so that your presentation is not disrupted.

Presentation Time

Presentation time is when you step into the spotlight. There are no retakes in a live show so step up and give your best performance.

As you work through your presentation, keep sight of where you are taking guests: on a journey toward the business, the booking, and the order. Having a basic structure mapped out will keep you on track as you put your games, tools, questions, stories, and commercials to work. But don't be so rigid that you can't adapt to your audience's interests.

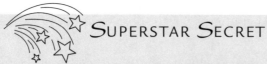 SUPERSTAR SECRET

Use a small notebook to record your best stories, games, anecdotes, and questions. Add to it when you conjure up new and better ways to present your products, bookings, and business. Flip through your notebook before each party and choose what you will use.

Invite your host to introduce you. All she needs to say is "Hi everyone. Let's get started. I want to thank you all for coming and introduce you to Nikki, our consultant." By sparing yourself the task of attracting guests' attention, you can focus on making a great first impression.

The start of the party is not the time to subject guests to a five-minute lecture on your company history or founders' vision. If your first few minutes are flat, you'll deflate the mood quicker than you can pop a balloon. It's time to dazzle guests so they think, "This is going to be great. I'm glad I came."

I suggest saying, "Hi everyone. Thank you for being here. I'm so glad that you made it and I can't wait for you to experience our amazing products. But first, let's thank Ellen for inviting us all into her home."

Thanking your host for "inviting us all into her home" includes you as a guest, not an outsider.

Hand her a beautifully wrapped thank-you gift as your first bookings commercial. You may like to add, "You're going to love it. I've had hosts who have booked a party just for the gift."

Or you can say, "It's a gift that we reserve exclusively for our hosts. So don't look for it on the order form. You have to host a party to get one."

If the gift your company provides is not especially exciting, you can substitute it with a better gift or let the wrapping work its magic. The recognition is worth more than the value of the gift.

Set a positive tone by being generous at the start of the party. Say, "Who feels lucky? Did you remember to bring your invitation? That's great, because we're about to draw our first winner. If the sticker on the front of your invitation matches the one I draw, it's going to be you! But you have to be here to win. So, if I don't draw an exact match, we'll draw again."

As the winner chooses her gift, say, "One of the best parts of hosting your own party is knowing your friends will win free gifts. Enjoying your own free shopping spree is the other."

Point to your party bags and say, "Who loves to shop? Everything you need to earn your own free shopping spree is in this bag. I'll tell you more about it later but, meanwhile, if you're already thinking you want your own party, make sure one of these bags has your name on it."

Hold up your calendar and say, "My party calendar has all my available dates highlighted. All you have to do is find a date that suits you and it's yours."

Draw attention to your star dates by saying, "You will see that some of the dates are marked with a star. Star dates mean extra gifts. But there aren't many, so you have to be quick to spot one, because the first person to write her name on that date wins."

If you prefer not to use the star dates, say, "And the best part is, if you book a party before I ask you to, you'll get this extra gift!"

Hold up a gift as you hand your calendar to the nearest guest so she can choose a date or pass it on.

SUPERSTAR SECRET

For more ideas on how to add variety to your booking commercials, see Chapter 5, "Create a Bookings Bonanza."

Hold up two pens and say, "You may be wondering why you have two pens. It's so that you can use the blue pen to mark products you are most interested in and the green pen for products you may be interested in, or that you think may be a little over your budget. I have some more news about that later."

"Does everyone have an order form? You'll also notice that some products are highlighted. They're the ones that I'll be focusing on tonight [are our best sellers/are on special right now/are my top personal picks]."

Now is a good time to play a game to reveal a top prospect. There is a wealth of games to choose from in Chapter 15, "It Pays to Play," including my surefire booking game "Icebreaker."

Pop the prize into one your business bags, and when you congratulate the winner, say, "Congratulations, you win [this amazing hand cream] plus all you need to know to start your own party plan business."

Hold up your guest slips and say, "I have plenty more gifts.

Make sure you fill in your guest draw slip so you can be in the next lucky guest draw."

Briefly share your story, keeping it to a one-minute maximum. You can say a lot in sixty seconds if you choose your words carefully:

"Has anyone ever dreamed of owning her own business? I know I did but I never thought it would happen. I thought it would cost too much and I was nervous about being on my own if things didn't work out. Then my best friend started selling these fabulous spa products and I hosted a party for her.

"But I still didn't think about joining. It was only when she called to say she had won a cruise that I thought, 'That's my kind of job.' That was a little over a year ago and right now I'm working toward earning a cruise to the Bahamas. But the best part is that I finally achieved my dream of owning my own business.

"So if your dreams are bigger than your paycheck, take a business bag home with you and find out how you can join us on our next cruise."

Or you can say:

"I started this business when my children were small. I love being a mom but I love working, too. I was the first of my friends to start a family and I remember them talking about a book they had all read and thinking, 'The only book I've read in the last six months, probably a hundred times, is *The Very Hungry Caterpillar.*' I felt isolated and I didn't like not having my own money. All that changed when I started my business.

"So, if you're a mom who wants to have the best of both worlds, take one of these business bags home with you so you can read more about how to be a mom and own your own business."

Switch to a different angle if you're not seeing the lights go on:

"My husband calls this my 'bling job' because the first thing I bought with my earnings was this ring. But the extra money has made a huge difference to us. It's taken the pressure off my husband, for a start. He has a good job but our money always used to run out before our week did.

"My party business pays for things we didn't used to be able to afford, like our weekly 'date night,' and we just bought a new car. Does anyone else here want a lifestyle that's bigger than her paycheck?"

Don't get so carried away with your story that you forget *why* you are sharing it. The fastest route to a new recruit is to trigger as many of these responses as you can:

* ✳ "I could do this!"
* ✳ "I'd love to do something like this!"
* ✳ "Maybe it's time I did something about my job."
* ✳ "This sounds like the perfect job for me."
* ✳ "This sounds like my dream job."

If you're not sure how to create your story, try filling the blanks in this sentence:

"I *was* _____ *but*_____ *so* _____."

"I *was* a loan officer for a bank *but* I got tired of all the petty politics, *so* when I learned about this business, I knew it would be perfect for me. My only regret is I didn't do it sooner."

Anyone who hates game playing at work will think, "Ka-ching!"

If you're working full-time *and* running your business, complete this sentence:

"I *am* _____ *but* _____ *so* _____."

"I *am* a physiotherapist *but* I could never afford to travel on my income. *So* I started doing parties. My parties are my travel money. I'm saving to take my mom on a trip back to Italy. She can't wait to catch up with family she hasn't seen in twenty years and I can't wait to shop till I drop. Who loves to travel?"

You don't have to share your whole story at one time. You can introduce different parts of it at different times. You could follow the previous story with this:

"What I love most about this business is not having to ask, 'Can I afford it?' when I want something. If I really want it, I book more parties so I can pay for it. Who loves to shop?"

Learn to encourage feedback by asking questions at the end of every story:

"I'm a mom but I do parties to help pay the bills and so that my husband and I can leave the kids with grandma and go on a trip once a year. My company offers an incentive trip every year, and working toward earning it keeps me motivated. The kids love it too because they get spoiled rotten at Grandma's. Who has a job that comes with a free vacation every year?"

Guests will be ready to hear about your products, but don't forget: Less is more! Aim for maximum impact in minimum time by leaving out the details and illustrating your products with vivid word pictures:

* "These brownies will melt in your mouth."
* "This fragrance will transport you to a tropical island."

* "Add these salts to your bath and you will feel like you're floating in silk."

* "Once you try one of our saucepans, you will want to switch all your saucepans. The difference in the quality of the food will amaze you."

* "Your skin will look and feel five years younger."

Don't forget to add a personal endorsement:

"Once I started using these products, I didn't want to try anything else. That's why I decided to sell them."

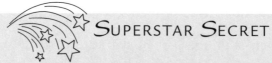 Superstar Secret

If you are selling skin care products, don't let a bad skin day steal your confidence. You can always joke, "This is what happens when I use our competitors' products."

Don't be tempted to oversell. The more you say, the less guests will listen and the secret is to explain what your products will do, not what they are:

"One week on our detox program and you'll feel like you've been on vacation."

"This lavender oil is so pure and concentrated that one drop will ease away all your tension. Add a drop to each temple when you go to bed and you won't be awake all night fretting when you want to be sleeping."

In the same way, talk about the host rewards, not how to host a party:

"Wait until you see what you get when you host your own party."

Using your imagination to come up with interesting suggestions will stretch your sales. If you sell books, talk about how a specific title makes a great potty book, car book, or book for grandma's library.

Place tabs in your catalogs to mark products that you will be talking about so guests can easily find them. You can turn that into a game. See "Fast Finger" and other sales games in Chapter 15.

Remind guests about the highlighted products on their order form, and to use both their pens, one for "musts" and the other for "maybes."

Learn to ask questions before you offer solutions:

"Who hasn't yet found the perfect skin care? I tried everything and then a friend recommended this brand. My skin felt different immediately."

Remember to keep stoking the booking and business fires. Most party planners don't talk nearly enough about bookings and the business and then they wonder why they're not getting enough bookings and business leads. You can't toy with those topics and expect results. You have to integrate them throughout your entire presentation.

Try merging business bids into your product presentation:

"When you become a consultant, you'll get this pendant in your Starter Kit."

"I actually have two jobs: selling this beautiful silver jewelry and helping other women start their own businesses."

In the same way, you can combine your booking and business bids:

"I hosted a party and received more than $150 in free products. That's when the light went on. I thought, 'My friends would love free jewelry,' so I signed on and asked my friends to host a party for me. When they saw what they got for helping me get started, they were lining up to be my first hosts."

The fastest way to light a fire is with fire, so share your enthusiasm and experiences:

"People often ask me what the best part of this job is and I have to say . . . everything. I've never had so much fun and I've never felt so happy with my job."

"The best part is I get to deduct all my expenses off my taxes."

"As women, we give so much and one of the things I love most about this job is the appreciation and recognition we get."

Or you can say:

"I went to a party and was blown away by what the consultant was saying. I thought, if even half of it is true, I want to do this."

What matters is that you are sincere. If you're working part-time, say so:

"I am still teaching but my goal is to do this full-time."

If you are new, say so:

"I'm still learning, but the training and support have been amazing."

Give your business meaning beyond the financial rewards. If you are selling do-it-yourself tools say:

"When I discovered that most of my friends were like me and had no idea how to do basic repairs or maintenance around our homes, I decided to make it my business. What I love about my job is I'm showing women how to be independent. It's empowering to know you don't have to rely on others."

Look for hints that show you someone is interested. To the guest who is being attentive, say,

"Thanks for being so interested. I'm guessing you love scrapbooking as much as I do."

 SUPERSTAR SECRET

A fun way to showcase your business is to take a few simple props to the party and hold them up when you talk about the many benefits newcomers will enjoy:

✻ **Small tiara:** "When was the last time your baby said, 'Thanks, mom, great job!' when you changed his diaper? What you'll love about this business is the recognition you get."

✻ **Christmas ornament:** "Who would love a debt-free Christmas this year? Helping your family and friends do their Christmas shopping is a great way to earn cash for Christmas."

✻ **Mickey Mouse toy:** "Last year we realized a family dream of a Disney vacation. The memories are going to last a lifetime and I paid for it all with my parties. If you'd love to take your family to Disney World, you should think about doing what I do."

✻ **Credit card:** "Did you know the average family spends one-third of their income on interest payments? That's how it used to be for me, but now I pay my credit card bill every month by doing parties. I love being debt free, and if that sounds good to you, too, we should talk."

* **Small box of cereal:** "How would you like to get your groceries free every week? One party a week pays my grocery bill."

* **Dollar bills:** "Anyone who says money doesn't buy happiness doesn't know where to shop. If you're looking for extra cash, we're looking for you."

Or say, "I joined because I love meeting new people and because I love having my own money."

* **Toy car:** "I had never even driven a new car until I earned one through my company's car program. Now I drive a red Mustang convertible. I just love it! Anyone want to take it for a test drive?"

Imagine sitting across the table talking about the business after your prospect has taken your company-provided car for a spin.

Don't shy away from talking about fears that hold people back from starting. You will always have their attention when you talk about what's on their minds:

"How many of you think you can't sell? That's exactly what I thought. But when I saw how much people loved our jewelry, I realized it was more about sharing than selling. Parties are great because everyone gets to try the jewelry on and get instant feedback from their friends."

You'll gather valuable information by keeping your ears open. Look for questions that indicate interest.

Question: "How did you get started?"

Answer: "I went to a party and just loved it. I never thought I would end up being a consultant but I'm glad I did. This is by far the best job I have ever had."

Question: "How did you learn about it all?"

Answer: "I remember thinking the same thing. Learning is the fun part. We have the most amazing training program and it's ongoing. I never felt that I had to know everything at the beginning. I just started doing parties and learned as I went."

Question: "How much do you make?"

Answer: "My parties average around $500 and I earn 30 percent of that. Our company even pays for the host gifts, so I earn about $150 a party. This is the first job I've ever had that I would do even if I didn't get paid."

Question: "Are there many people selling this around here?"

Answer: "Everyone loves our products so we have a few consultants in the area. But we could have ten times the number we have, and we're always looking for the right people to join us. Why don't you come to our next meeting? We meet for around ninety minutes and it's a great way to learn about the business without feeling obligated. Plus you can meet some of the other consultants. They're a fun group and they'd love you."

Question: "What did you do before?"

Answer: "I'm actually a registered nurse but nothing would persuade me to do that again. Working shifts takes its toll after a few years. I just love having my own business and I love helping others become self-employed, too. What do you do?"

Question: "Is this your full-time job?"

Answer: "It sure is. It didn't start out that way. I was working full-time as a loan officer but I quit as soon as I began earning more doing parties than I earned at the bank. Plus, I'm working half the hours. Now I wonder why it took me so long."

Or, "Actually I am a full-time mom but my parties are my 'me' time. The money I make pays for things I'd feel guilty buying if I didn't have my own income."

Make sure you are asking questions that will reveal guests on your prospect-shopping list:

"Has anyone been a party planner?"

"Who has been in direct selling?"

"Who was a cheerleader at school?"

"Who would have loved to be a cheerleader but didn't have the nerve to try out?"

"Who would describe themselves as artistic?"

"Who has the worst job [or the worst boss] ever?"

"Who would quit their job tomorrow if they could?"

Keep the pace moving. If you sense guests' attention is wavering, change the pace—introduce a game, award a prize, or bring out a hidden item. The more fun they're having, the more attentive they'll be and the more likely it is that they'll buy, book, and consider the business.

CHAPTER 12

The Grand Finale

Now welcome to closing time. No matter how many times you've spoken about the products, the bookings, and the business during your presentation, you have to close on all three.

Closing Time

Thank everyone for coming, ask if anyone has any last questions, and say, "Let me take you through the order form."

Demonstrate the same confidence you showed during your presentation by saying "*When* you place your order" not "*If* you place an order."

Try running your sales, booking, and business closes together:

"Before I finish, does anyone have any questions? Just a reminder, your order will be shipped direct to Ellen [or you] by Monday next week. Deciding what you want to order will be easy if you've marked your favorites with the blue pen.

But if your wish list is bigger than your budget and you've marked some items in green, why not get those free by hosting your own party?

"All you have to do is invite a few friends over. I'll do the rest, and remember, you'll receive a free gift just for booking, and 10 percent of your party sales toward your free shopping spree—isn't that awesome? But there's more. For every guest who books at your party, you can select any one item at half price. I always tell my hosts to order the most expensive item because that means you save more. Why not?"

Remember to encourage guests to book your closest dates. The closer they book, the less likely hosts are to cancel:

"Don't forget that you receive an extra gift for booking a star date, as Ruby has already done tonight. Thanks Ruby, I can't wait to do your party. I think I have one star date still available. Let me check. Yes, Saturday the 12th is still free. Anyone prefer a weekend brunch party to a midweek evening?"

Or you can say:

"It definitely pays to book in the next three weeks because June is our host-appreciation month. You receive the Fourth of July candles absolutely free, on top of your regular host rewards."

Now move straight to your business close:

"Is anyone thinking that it sounds too good to be true? That's what I thought when I went to my first party. The amazing host rewards were one of the reasons I decided to become a consultant. I thought, 'Everyone will want to host a party with rewards like this!'"

Here is another way to combine your product, booking, and business closes:

"While you're deciding what products you want to order, let me run through your options. You can order everything you want now, or you can order some products now and do what Ellen did—host your own party. Apart from the fun, the rewards you get are amazing. Or you can do what I did and start your own party plan business. You won't believe the support you get."

Make a general business invitation that includes everyone and a guest who has fallen under your radar may come forward:

"I really appreciate you all being here tonight. It's been fun getting to know you. And here's something I invite you to think about: How would you like to do what I do? It's a great way to own a business and you get all the training and support you need. Even if you haven't thought of doing something like this before, think about it. I had absolutely no sales experience when I started and I can honestly say that I have never had so much fun making money."

If you're holding guests' attention, keep sharing information about how simple it is to get started:

"You may be wondering how you get started. Most people don't believe how easy it is. There are basically just three steps.

"As soon as you sign an Independent Consultant Agreement, you receive your Starter Kit and can start earning immediately. The Starter Kit costs $XXX but the company contributes twice that in products and business supplies, so you're already ahead.

"Next, you let your friends and family know about the exciting gifts they'll get for hosting one of your practice parties. Our personal contacts are usually our first customers, hosts, and even consultants. It's all pretty exciting and the best part is you can start earning while you're still learning. You will earn 30 percent or more on your sales, right from the start.

"The fun part is training, where you learn how to build your business beyond your friends and family. The biggest thing for me was realizing I didn't have to know it all. I'm still learning and the company supports us with amazing incentives in our first few weeks. So if you're looking for part-time work, a full-time business, or even a casual job, take one of these business bags home and I'd be happy to set up a time to talk."

Don't oversell. If you are relaxed, your guests will relax. Keep it light and simple. If you oversell the business, you won't get many takers. Talk small, part-time, and now!

"Is anyone looking for part-time work before Christmas? If you did one party a week starting now you could earn $1,000 or more and we have a special training scheduled next week for our Santa-sellers. Would an extra $1,000 make a difference to your holidays?"

End your presentation by inviting guests to complete their guest slips:

"Thank you for being here tonight and for being such a great group. We're almost finished, so while you think about what you want to order, and hosting your own party, make sure you fill in your guest slip so we can draw our lucky winner. Who knows what they want already?"

Gather in the guest slips, thank your host, and congratulate those who have committed to a booking or appointment to talk about the business. Close your structured time on a high note by drawing one guest slip as your lucky last winner.

CHAPTER 13

Reap the Rewards

ONE-ON-ONE TIME IS WHEN YOU WILL reap the rewards of your planning, preparation, and superb presentation. It's time to close each guest on the order, the booking, and the business:

* Your primary goal is to turn each guest into your next recruit.

* Your next goal is to turn each guest into your next host.

* Your third goal is to turn each guest into a VIP Customer Club member.

Show an interest in what each guest orders, and regardless of how much they ordered, make them feel good about it:

* "Good choice."

* "That's one of my favorites."

* "That was one of the first products I bought."
* "That shade is perfect for you."

If you want to drive your customers to your Web site or to sign them up for AutoShip, make it easy by giving them a step-by-step guide and a reward if they place their first order within a month. An offer with an expiration date will always get a better response than an open-ended offer:

"Not only will you save 10 percent by enrolling as a Preferred Customer, by placing your first order before [date] you receive a free [product]."

The deadline also gives you an excuse to make a friendly reminder call: "I'm calling to make sure you don't miss out on your free gift."

One-on-one time isn't over until your guest says so. Until that time, keep moving forward by making helpful suggestions. It's not your job to guess what your customer can afford. Give your customers credit for knowing what's in their wallet.

If she orders one item, suggest a complementary product:

"Did you see these new embellishments? They make a perfect match for the cardstock you chose."

"If you love the bracelet, you should think about buying the earrings while they're on special."

If she is close to ordering a collection, point out the value of adding another item:

"Did you see the savings you get when you purchase the entire collection?"

Never assume your customer has seen a special offer:

"Did you see that the stamp and the ink come as a duo? It's cheaper than buying them individually."

"Do you realize that your total qualifies you to buy an extra bonus item?"

Point out any items you have highlighted:

"Did you take a look at the items I highlighted? They are on special this month only so it's your only chance to buy them at that price."

Refer back to her order form:

"Did you manage to get everything you wanted, or are there still items on your wish list?"

If just one guest at each party accepts your recommendations, your sales will increase significantly over a year.

Review the guest slips but invite all guests to join your VIP Customer Club, whether or not they checked that box.

You may like to use your VIP Customer Club to up-sell:

"You've ordered $64 worth of goodies today and if you order more than $70 you automatically get upgraded to my VIP Customer Club. It's definitely worth it because you're the first to hear about new products and specials; plus you get VIP-only specials, free samples, and invites to our amazing product launches."

Ask for the booking. No matter how hard you have to work

for it, it will be easier than cold calling the next day. Look for the signals that could lead to a booking.

If she says, "I love it but I'll save it for next time," you can say, "Why not get it free?"

If she says, "I'll order that at Tiffany's party," you can say, "That's fantastic. Have you thought about having your own party so you can get free products, too?"

If you are smart, you will think of every party as an opportunity meeting and not hesitate to invite every guest to join:

"How do you feel about joining us? I'd love to work with you."

Ask questions that invite a response:

"Where would you like to go from here?"

"Are you thinking, 'I could do this'?"

"I saw your eyes light up when I talked about my car. How do you feel about going for it? I'm happy to help you."

Invite your best prospects directly:

"You are exactly who we are looking for."

"You would definitely fit in with our group."

The number one reason a prospect won't meet with you is that it's easier to say no on the spot than risk being pressured. Always offer an escape route so a prospect feels comfortable:

"Party plan isn't for everyone but it may be fun to find out if it's for you."

Have a next step ready for those who are interested but not ready to move forward:

"Our next new consultant training is on Saturday. If you decide before then, you can start right away."

"We have an 'It Pays to Party' workshop every month, where you learn everything you need to get started. It runs for about ninety minutes and it's a lot of fun. What do you think?"

"Why don't we meet for coffee? I would love to get to know you better."

"Why don't you come to a party with me? I love bringing guests along to see how it's done and I have a booking next week less than a mile from here."

Keep your tone light and relaxed. If you apply pressure or make party plan sound complicated, you are more likely to talk them out of the business than into it. Most of our decisions are not black and white. How you connect with guests on a personal level could easily tilt them away from a no to a yes. There is no reason to sign your prospects up on the spot. Use the time you have with them to take your relationship to the next step.

Close your one-on-one time depending on the decision each guest makes.

To casual customers, you can say:

"I really appreciate your order, and I promise I'll look after you. The first thing I will do is call and make sure you are happy. I'm sure you will be, but I want to know for sure. Then I'll call you once a month to see if you want anything. But please don't wait for me to call you. You can call me anytime. Here's my card [or fridge magnet, key ring, sticky label for your calendar]. It has my contact details on it."

To guests who have joined your VIP Customer Club, you can say:

"Welcome to my VIP Customer Club. You can expect your first newsletter within two weeks and there is always an exciting offer included with it so open it as soon as you can."

 SUPERSTAR SECRET

Check that you have her correct e-mail address. Some e-mail addresses can be hard to decipher and it's easier to correct errors on the spot than wait until an e-mail bounces back.

Set a time and place for your first coaching call for guests who have booked a party.

Set a time and a place to meet for an appointment with your prospective consultant.

Plan your one-on-one time wisely to avoid spending too much time with one guest at the expense of others. No matter how excited you are about one particular guest, keep it moving so each guest has her turn for your undivided attention. You will have plenty of time to continue the conversation over the next few days.

CHAPTER 14

Reward and Recruit Your Host

TURN YOUR ATTENTION BACK to your host when you have spent time with each guest. Congratulate her on a great party, total her sales and bookings, and help her finalize her host rewards. Remember to check her "Host Challenge" card (see Figure 1 on page 163) and reward her for completing all squares or any line.

Be excited about what she has earned. Happy hosts book more parties, invite more guests, give you referrals . . . and become consultants.

If your host has just missed a reward level, offer to leave her party open for twenty-four hours so she can top up her sales or bookings. Leaving it open longer than that will encourage procrastination. A little urgency will keep your host motivated, and the more parties you have open at any time, the more complicated your job becomes.

Make sure she understands what happens next—including collecting payments and chasing down outside orders.

Tell her which guests have expressed interest in the business and say that you will keep her posted. Share who has booked a party and say, "I hope I'll see you there. It will be your turn to sit back and relax."

Congratulate her on becoming a member of your VIP Host Club, as that means she will be the first to hear about your most exciting invitations and offers.

The last thing to do as you leave the house is to thank your host and make a sincere compliment about her party:

"I wish all my hosts were like you."

"That was fun. You have such great friends."

"Your home is stunning."

"You have definitely been one of my favorite hosts."

Don't leave garbage at her home, ask her to assist in the cleanup, or have her help you to your car. Leave her with a lasting impression of how easy it will be to host her next party.

Your relationship with your host doesn't stop when the party is over. Call her within twenty-four hours and say, "Thanks for being such a wonderful host. Did you have fun? Are you excited about all the wonderful products you earned? I think we did a great job working together."

Compliment her on what went especially well:

"Yours was my best party this month, thanks to you."

"It may have been a small party, but what we lacked in numbers we made up for in fun. I was able to spend more time with your friends."

Don't do all the talking. Ask her how she felt the party went and check to see if she has any extra orders or questions. Remind her to ask all guests who have not booked a party if they are interested in doing so when she delivers their orders, and sweeten the deal by offering her a reward if they agree.

If you will be sending all guest orders to the host, explain that you will send her an e-mail confirming who ordered, what they ordered, how many boxes to expect, and the approximate delivery date.

Suggest that she check everything to make sure that nothing is broken or faulty and that she keep the packing slips until she has delivered all her orders to her guests. Keep her informed if hiccups arise. If any items are on back order or are out of stock, advise her of this immediately.

Make your final host call when you are confident that every guest has her order to check that everyone is happy. Thank her again for making her party a success and delivering all products safely. If she has not booked another party or signed up, you can say, "I hope this isn't the last time we'll be talking. Can I keep in touch and call you when something special comes up?"

Recruiting Your Host

Your host is a top candidate for the business and halfway toward becoming a consultant already. She has friends, she enjoys parties, she loves the products, and she can organize a party. Industry statistics suggest that one in every five hosts will sign on as a consultant, and the more successful her party is, the more likely it is your host will be one of them.

From the moment she books her party, you must do everything you can to show your host that your job is exciting, rewarding, and profitable.

After her second coaching session, send her a business pack with a handwritten note that says, "I would love to help you do what I do. I know you'd be amazing and you'll be surprised at how easy it is to get started. Take a look and let me know what you think."

Build her confidence throughout her coaching and party with sincere compliments. If she feels good about her performance as a host, she will be more receptive to the idea of becoming a consultant:

> "I wish all my hosts were as organized [much fun or popular] as you."

If you do as much listening as you do talking, you will learn a lot about her during coaching. Use this information to tailor your sponsoring commercials. If she loves to travel, talk about how you love working toward a free trip every year and how exciting it is when the company announces the destination.

If she has young children, talk about how much you love having a job that fits so well with being a mom and how you think that it's as important to balance "mom time" and "me time" as it is to balance work and play.

If she's a career woman, talk about how the business can be worked part-time, or say, "Do you ever think about going out on your own?" Or, "Have you ever thought about using your skills to start your own business?"

Is it important to try to sponsor your host before or during her party? My vote is no. There's no rush. The fact that she booked with you shows she likes you. Relax and let her enjoy her party.

But if it feels right to do so, approach your host during her party.

The few minutes you have with your host before guests arrive are a good time to sow this little sponsoring seed: "You've been great to work with. I've loved planning your party with you. I have an idea: Tonight, watch what I do and see how much fun my job is. I think you would be great at it."

You can also talk to your host after her party, while she is excited: "I would love to work with you. You're fun and I think you could do really well."

Express your confidence in her: "You did such a great job of being a host. I think you're a natural."

SUPERSTAR SECRET

A great way to approach your host after the party is to ask, "How do you think your party went?" When she gives you feedback, say, "Do you know what the hardest part was?"

No doubt her curiosity will be piqued, and that's when you can say, "It was the part that you did. All I did was turn up and have fun. It was great meeting your friends and they seemed to love everything. But that's how party plan works. The host does most of the work and we make the money. I think you'd love doing parties and I'm sure just about everyone who came would book a party for you."

If her guests have booked parties, you have an even more appealing offer to make: "I have an idea. If you start now, I will give you the two bookings I got tonight. You need only six parties and you're in business."

Or you can say, "You have a choice to make. It's fine to join later, but if you do it now, we can use Nikki's and Amanda's parties as your apprentice parties. I'll still do them but you can come along to help and I'll give you 20 percent of party sales toward your Starter Kit."

If you haven't yet given your host a business pack, you can say, "In fact, I got so excited thinking about having you on our team that I brought some information for you to look at. Party plan isn't for everyone, but if you like having fun and making money at the same time, it may be worth taking a look."

Or you can say, "As soon as we met, I thought, 'She would make a great consultant.' But I didn't want to distract you from your party. Now I'm even more convinced you'd be great. Now that you've seen how it works, how do you feel about becoming a consultant? I would love to work with you. I think you're a natural."

Make sure you have an agreement ready in case the answer is yes. If your host is eager to sign, she will want to know what her next steps will be. Talk about how she can start with a Launch Party and a few friends who are willing to host one of her first parties. Build her confidence up by pointing out that her friends had a great time and will want to help her:

> "I'm pretty sure Kayla and Nurit would host a party for you. They loved the products and placed the biggest orders."

If your host is interested but not ready to commit, schedule a time to meet, or invite her to an event where she can experience the business without pressure or obligation.

A host continues to be a hot business prospect whether she signs immediately or not. At any time she may change her mind, or her circumstances. She may lose her job, tire of her hours, or be planning to start a family soon. The pilot light is always burning—it's your job to make sure you are there to ignite it when the right time comes. A party plan superstar never thinks never!

CHAPTER 15

It Pays to Play

GAMES ARE A FANTASTIC TOOL to include in your party plan tool kit. They can break the ice, introduce a little fun and excitement to the party, and help guests relax. But that's not the main reason you play them. Games are the easiest way to identify guests on your prospect-shopping list and give you valuable insights into their personalities:

* Who uses your type of products? She's a top customer, host, and business prospect.

* Who has hosted or attended parties? Past behavior is a surefire way to predict future behavior.

* Who is having the most fun? Fun-loving people are great candidates to become hosts and consultants.

* Who is the most competitive? They will love the recognition and rewards that come with a party plan business.

* Who is talking the most? They may be the enthusiasts you are looking for.

* Who is participating wholeheartedly? Talk to them about the fun and friendships that come with a party plan business.

* Who is taking part reluctantly or halfheartedly? They may be disinterested or distracted. Don't dismiss them as prospects. Find out more before you decide how to approach them.

These tips will help you make the most of the games you incorporate into your parties:

* Play a maximum of two games at each party.

* Don't waste time playing games that do not move you closer to identifying a sale, a booking, or a business lead.

* Choose a few simple games when you are new and gradually introduce more games as you gain confidence.

* By all means experiment, but introduce games that you feel comfortable with. You need only a few tried-and-true favorites to achieve your host- and prospect-shopping objectives.

* Rotate games so guests can see that you are not a one-trick pony. A party is not fun if it is predictable.

* Make it all about the fun. Don't give the impression that you are trying to influence a specific outcome.

* Never attempt to coax a reluctant guest into participating. The more relaxed you are, the more relaxed guests will be.

* Introduce your first game early. Being generous with gifts and rewards at the start of the party will warm guests to you and your presentation.

* Wrap each prize with a host or business brochure, or pop prizes into your business or party bags. When you hand them to winners, say, "Congratulations, you have won . . . and there's some information about our host rewards [business] that I think you'll find interesting."

* Keep your costs down by stocking up with prizes when they are on special or by snapping up bargains when your local retailers hold clearance sales.

BOOKING GAMES

LUCKY DIP!

Preparation: Arrange gifts of varying shapes and sizes in a basket.

Play: Pick up the basket and say, "Who enjoys surprises?" Explain that anyone who books a party within the next five minutes can choose a gift from your basket. You may even like to set a timer to build excitement.

MYSTERY ENVELOPE!

Preparation: Print vouchers for the following rewards:

"10 percent off your order today!"
"$10 cash to spend at your party!"
"Choose any gift from my basket!"

Place the vouchers inside three separate envelopes and write the dates you wish to book first (i.e., your closest available dates) on the outside of each envelope.

Play: Show the envelopes and talk about the rewards that may be inside each one. Explain that the first guest to book a party on the date written on the envelope wins the reward inside it.

DEAL OR NO DEAL!

Preparation: Prepare six small boxes, numbered one to six, and randomly place the following rewards inside:

* Three "instant gift" vouchers
* One "$10 gift voucher to spend at your party"
* One "$20 gift voucher to spend at your party"
* One "$30 gift voucher to spend at your party"

Play: Set the boxes with the numbers facing the guests and ask, "Who wants to play 'Deal or No Deal'?"

Explain that the odds are 50 percent that they will receive an instant gift and 50 percent that they will draw a party. By playing, guests agree to book a party if their box contains a voucher that can only be redeemed at their party.

Give each player a turn to select a numbered box and hold it up as you review the rewards that may be inside. Asking "Which reward do you hope is in your box?" will help build suspense and encourage interaction.

The fun is in the anticipation so don't open the box too fast.

NB: You can involve all guests by encouraging them to guess what they think is in the box before you reveal its contents.

YOU GUESSED IT!

Preparation: Create a rewards board with cutouts of the products on your host's wish list and products you want to promote, with the prices showing.

At the end of your one-on-one time, tally up the party total quickly so guests don't start wandering off. Do not reveal the total to your host.

Play: Invite your host to the front to choose her free products one by one. Remove the pictures from the board as she does.

Guests take turns guessing when the host has reached her rewards total by calling out "No guess!" or "Guess!" as she removes each item. Guests who call "No guess!" stay in the game for another chance to win. The guest who calls "Guess!" closest to your host's exact reward total is the winner.

TAKE A CHANCE!

Preparation: Assemble two dice, twelve envelopes (numbered one through twelve), seven mini prizes, three grand prizes, and four host reward brochures. Print twelve cards as follows:

* ❖ Seven cards that say "Congratulations! You have won a mini prize!"
* ❖ Four cards that say "Congratulations! Book your party and earn fantastic host rewards!"
* ❖ Three cards that say "Congratulations! You are a grand prize winner!"

Place one grand prize card in the envelope numbered two or twelve (as the odds of throwing those numbers are smaller) and place the remaining two grand prize cards aside for guests who choose to book a party before the game begins. Randomly place the other eleven cards in the remaining envelopes.

Play: Place the envelopes and prizes in front of the guests. Explain that some of the envelopes contain a mini prize card, some a party card, and one the grand prize card. Say, "If you win a prize, it's yours to keep. If you win a party card, you have to book a party."

Show the grand prize and ask, "Who doesn't like taking chances? If you book a party before we start throwing the dice, I will give you the grand prize regardless. If you intend to book a party anyway, this is the time to do it and I'll bring the grand prize to your party. Does anyone want to claim the guaranteed grand prize before we start?"

Invite guests one by one to take the guaranteed grand prize, keeping the tone playful and relaxed. Then say, "Who wants first throw of the dice?"

Each player then throws the dice and takes the envelope, without opening it, that corresponds to the number thrown. Guests who subsequently throw the same number try again.

When every player has an envelope, they open their envelopes simultaneously and reveal their prizes.

As you distribute the prizes, say to guests who drew party cards, "You are the biggest winners, because look what you get when you host a party," and then run through the host reward program.

PASS THE PARCEL!

Preparation: Wrap a gift with seven layers of paper.

Make up a poem that highlights the benefits of booking a party, or adapt the example that follows.

Hand the parcel to your host so she can start the ball rolling by passing the parcel to the guest who best fits the first verse of the poem. Each recipient removes a layer of wrap and passes the parcel to the guest who best fits the next verse you read out, until one guest unwraps the last layer to win the gift inside.

Pass the Parcel Poem

As our host I have great gifts for you.
But your guests can earn fun prizes, too.

Pass the parcel to the person who
Traveled the farthest to be with you.

Pass it on when you find the one
Who thinks shopping is such fun.
That when she's out, just can't resist
Adding more items to her list.

And now we'll find another guest
Who thinks winning is the best.
If you like gifts that come for free
Just be the first to call out "Me!"

When you book your party date
We'll have great fun, so please don't wait.
And now we'll find another guest
Who stands up taller than the rest!

Some of you have been a host
But who's the one who's done it most?
If you have been a host before
Add up quick, call out your score.

This party game is almost done.
We've nearly found the guest who's won.
Let's find the one we will delight.
Please pass the parcel three guests right!

We'll now unwrap the final layer.
The parcel stops with this one player.
Thanks for joining in the fun.
Congratulations! You're the one!

HOST CHALLENGE

Preparation: Photocopy the "Host Challenge" card (see Figure 1) or prepare a tic-tac-toe grid and add the following tasks in the grid and a note on the bottom about gifts hosts can win:

Figure 1: Host Challenge

Two+ orders before your party	Two+ bookings by close of party	Book another party within three months
Party held on original date	Ten+ guests attending	Guest list returned by ....
Three guests I've never met	Sales of $500+	Twelve+ guests attending

Earn a gift by completing any vertical, horizontal, or diagonal line. Complete all boxes and win a bonus gift.

Play: Introduce the "Host Challenge" game during your host's first coaching session.

If twelve or more guests attend, you can check both the ten+ and the twelve+ squares.

SPONSORING GAMES

ICEBREAKER!

Preparation: Pen and paper for each guest

Play: Explain that you will ask six questions, and guests will award themselves points for their answers. The guest with the most points wins.

The questions are:

Question one: "How many parties like this one have you been to in the past two years?"
Award one point per party.

Question two: "How many parties like this one have you been to in the past six months?"
Award two additional points for each party.

Question three: "Have you hosted a party for any company in the last two years?"
Award three points for each party hosted.

 ## SUPERSTAR SECRET

Show an extra interest in guests who have hosted parties. Ask, "Who was it with?" and make a positive comment in response:

"I know that company. Was it a great party?"

"I haven't heard of them but it sounds like fun."

"Did you earn lots of free products?"

Question four: "How many parties have you hosted in the last six months?"
Award three additional points for each party hosted.

SUPERSTAR SECRET

Ask your guests for the contact details of the consultant who did their party so that you can call her up and suggest you host a party for each other. Professional contacts are valuable. Once you build a database of other party planners, you can help each other. For example, join together to hold a holiday gift fair.

Question five: Tailor the next question to your products. For example:

* Jewelry: One point for every pair of earrings you own
* Cosmetics: One point for every lipstick you purchased this year
* Children's books: One point for each book you read to your children this week
* Scrapbooking, card making, and stamping: One point for each photo you have with you today [or displayed on your dresser]
* Candles: One point for every candle you lit this week [or month]
* Nutrition: One point for each nutritional supplement you take daily
* Cookware and foods: One point for each time your family sat together to share a meal this week
* Skin care: One point for each step in your daily skin care routine

NB: If a guest asks for clarification, try to answer in the affirmative. If she asks, "Do you count products twice if you use them day and night?" you can answer, "Absolutely."

Question Six: "Who has been a direct seller?"
Award five points.
Invite guests to tally their points and then do a count-

down to the guest who has the highest score. She is the winner, and the hottest prospect in the room. Take special note of all guests with a higher-than-average score, because they are excellent prospects, too.

SUPERSTAR SECRET

Ask guests who have been direct sellers, "Who were you with?" and offer a personal compliment:

"You come across as someone who would do really well at this."

"I can see it. You have such a bubbly personality."

CHOCOHOLIC DELIGHT!

Preparation: A box or bag of chocolates

Play: Explain that you love questions, because then you don't waste time talking about topics no one is interested in. Hold up the chocolates and say, "Who loves chocolate? If you ask any question about my business, you get chocolate." Segue each question into a commercial.

Question: "How many parties do you do each week?"

Answer: "Sometimes two and sometimes three. It's my choice when I want to work. There is more demand for our products before Valentine's Day, Mother's Day, and Christmas, so that's when I work more. Last year, my Christmas parties alone paid for our family trip to the Grand Canyon. It was an incredible family experience."

GOTCHA!

Preparation: A roll of tickets

Play: Every time you mention your company name, the first person to call out "Gotcha" takes a ticket. The duplicate ticket goes into a bag and you draw a lucky winner at the end of your presentation.

LEFT, RIGHT, LEFT!

Preparation: Create a story about your business using the words "left" and "right" as often as possible (or adapt the following example).

Play: As you read the script aloud, guests count how many times you say the words "right" or "left." For example, you could say:

"When I *left* my house tonight I was about to turn *right* out of my driveway before I realized I had *left* my catalogs behind. So I stopped the car, *left* the engine running, and headed *right* back inside.

"I searched *left* and *right* before I found the catalogs on the *left* side of the kitchen table, *right* where I had *left* them. I grabbed them, *left* the house, and headed *right* back to my car.

"As I live *right* around the corner from Stacey's house, I only had to turn *right* out of my driveway, take the first street on the *right*, turn *left*, and drive two blocks. I had *left* plenty of time so I made it *right* on time.

"I reached Stacey's house and turned *left* into her driveway. I was the first to arrive so I pulled as far as I could to the *right* to make room for someone else to park *right* next to me.

"Stacey had *left* the door open for me so I came *right* inside and started setting up my display, including the catalogs I had *left* behind. No sooner had I finished than people started arriving *right* and *left* and so now all that's *left* is to make sure we all have a great time."

NB: The correct answer in this example is twenty-seven.

PURSE SCRAMBLE!

Preparation: A roll of tickets

Play: Ask guests to set their handbags on their lap.

Invite guests to rummage through their handbags for items that start with each letter you call out. The first person to produce an item receives a ticket, with the duplicate going into the draw. "T" may produce a ticket or a telephone; "C" a calculator, chocolate, cell phone, or cash; "M" a mint or money. You can make the game more fun by accepting outrageous or creative answers.

To make it more challenging, invite guests to suggest a benefit of your business that matches each letter. Each suggestion earns an extra ticket and gives you a chance to share a commercial.

If a guest volunteers that "T" stands for time, say, "That's a brilliant one. I work when I want to, not to someone else's agenda."

If a guest volunteers that "M" stands for money, say, "That's the best part. I can earn a little or a lot, depending on what I want and how much time I have to work. With three children, I need to be flexible."

WHAT'S IN YOUR BAG?

Preparation: A roll of tickets

Play: Invite guests to rummage inside their handbag for the most unusual item they can find, and then invite them to explain why it was in there. Not only will you spot your best prospects from the creativity of their answers, you will have a talking point when you follow up with them.

SALES GAMES

ORDER AND WIN!

Preparation: A roll of tickets

Play: Guests earn one ticket for each item they order, regardless of its value. The more tickets they receive, the greater their chance of winning the draw. Introduce the game during your closing presentation and remind each guest individually during her one-on-one time.

As an alternative, offer guests a ticket for every $10 they spend.

BAG LADY!

This game will reveal guests with the most passion for your products.

Preparation: None

Play: Challenge guests to produce the highest number of items associated with your products from their handbag. For example, if you sell beauty products, you are sure to find someone whose bag is bulging with lipstick, mascara, and hand cream. If you have a tiebreaker, the guest with the most number of your brand wins.

WHO AM I?

Preparation: Create a simple questionnaire that is appropriate for your products, such as this one I created for a gourmet food company called Home Chef!

"Home Chef"

Check which one describes your cooking style:

- ❑ Creative: I love to experiment.
- ❑ Competent: I never follow recipes.
- ❑ Cautious: I meticulously follow the recipe.
- ❑ Conscientious: It's all about nutrition.
- ❑ Casual: Whatever I can find in the pantry.
- ❑ Convivial: I love to entertain.
- ❑ Convenience: My microwave is my best friend.
- ❑ Comfort: I'm a soup, meatloaf, mac and cheese chef.
- ❑ Competitive: I love to attempt ambitious recipes.
- ❑ Cook? I never use the words "I" and "cook" in the same sentence.

Play: Hand a questionnaire and pen to each guest and ask guests to check the description that best represents their cooking style. Invite them to share their answers. The game provides an entertaining interlude to the party, and it reveals insights into guests' personalities that will make one-on-one time and follow-up calls a breeze.

I'M A CELEBRITY!

Preparation: Make a note of popular movies or television series, especially the leading characters. During coaching, ask your host which show her guests are most likely to be watching.

Play: Invite guests to nominate the character they most resemble in looks or personality.

Alternative ways to play the game are:

Freestyle: Guests nominate any well-known person they resemble.

Spot the celebrity: Guests nominate a well-known person who they think another guest resembles. Popular vote determines who came up with the best suggestion.

The next two games will help to fill time if you are waiting for latecomers. Although it is always best to start on time, you are never in complete control and you may as well use the time productively by engaging with guests and learning about their personalities.

GETTING TO KNOW YOU!

Preparation: Print a questionnaire for each guest.

Play: Distribute this questionnaire and invite everyone to find a guest who matches each clue and to write that guest's name in as the answer:

* Has two children under seven
* You have never met
* You have known the longest
* Lives the closest to you
* Was once a cheerleader (Prospect-shopping alert! Pay special attention as former cheerleaders are always hot prospects.)
* Traveled farthest to be here
* Adapt the question to your products. For example, who is wearing the most interesting jewelry?

The first guest to complete all questions wins.

HOST WITH THE MOST!

Preparation: None

Play: Invite guests to take turns sharing a quality of the host that they admire:

> "I admire Stella because she is always there for me when I need her."
>
> "I admire Stella's style. She always looks amazing."

FAST FINGER!

Preparation: Choose an item in your catalog to focus on.

Play: When all guests have a catalog in their hands, you can say, "I am going to give you a clue that will identify one item in the catalog. The first person to find it and call out the page number wins."

When the item has been found, take a few seconds to talk about why you drew their attention to it.

TEAM MEETING GAMES

TEAM TIC-TAC-TOE!

Preparation: Focus team members on nine key business-building activities by preparing a tic-tac-toe grid that features key tasks they must perform within a specific time frame. Purchase a punch or stamp that you will use to acknowledge that each task has been completed.

Play: Give all team members a tic-tac-toe card. Run through the tasks they have to complete and the time frame they have to complete them.

NB: Attending meetings will keep guests motivated and focused. Stipulate that they must attend a meeting to have their card punched or stamped.

When they complete a horizontal, vertical, or diagonal line, they win a small reward. If they complete all squares, they win a bonus gift.

Variation: This game is the perfect way to focus team members on what they need to do to achieve an important promotion, such as the annual incentive trip. Dividing a long-term incentive into weekly or monthly segments will help them focus on what they need to do now.

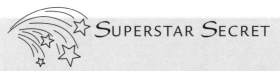

SUPERSTAR SECRET

Work smart by rewarding team members with training or business tools, such as a CD, a book, or business cards, as prizes.

Your time is another work-smart reward. Your undivided attention over lunch or dinner where an achieving team member can enjoy one-on-one mentoring and recognition will make a highly effective reward.

IN TO WIN!

Preparation: A roll of tickets, a large glass jar, and a bundle of dollar bills

Play: Ask team members, one by one, how many parties they have held for the month. Put one dollar in the jar for each party they report.

Each team member receives one ticket for attending the meeting and one for each party they report. The more parties they have done, the more tickets they will receive and the greater chance they have of winning. When all parties have been reported, draw one ticket and the winner takes home the cash.

Variation: Hand out one extra ticket for every $100 in sales each consultant has achieved, and ten extra tickets for each new recruit they sign up.

FASCINATION!

Preparation: None

Play: Pair team members up and give them sixty seconds to discover an interesting fact about each other. Each one has ten seconds to introduce her partner. The pair who reveals the most fascinating facts about each other wins.

    Variation: Challenge each partner to find out something that no one knows about the other and reveal it to the group.

TRUE OR FALSE!

Preparation: None

Play: Invite each team member to share one true and one false fact about herself. Other team members vote on which fact is true and which one is false.

INTRODUCTIONS!

Preparation: None

Play: Invite team members to introduce themselves, adding a one-word description of their best quality that starts with the same letter as their first name, for example, Enthusiastic Ellen, Determined Deb, Fearless Frances, Hard-working Hannah.

THE PERFECT PARTY!

Preparation: None

Play: Split team members into groups and invite each group to brainstorm one key element of a perfect party:

* Dynamic displays
* Persuasive presentations
* Booking bonanzas
* Spectacular sponsoring
* Captivating closes

Nominate a team captain to oversee the discussion and ensure that everyone has a chance to contribute. Give each group ten minutes to brainstorm before inviting team captains to share the best ideas that were presented to the group with everyone at the meeting.

SHOW AND SHARE!

Preparation: E-mail all team members and ask them to bring their "best big idea" to the meeting. Bring sticky notes and pens to the meeting.

Play: Ask team members to write their best big idea on a sticky note and paste it on the wall around the room as they arrive, to form a "best big idea" gallery. During the meeting, invite team members to walk around the room searching for their next best big idea.

Hand out more sticky notes, and ask team members to write their next best big idea on it. They can take the note home after the meeting and stick it on their mirror where it will remind them to use the idea every day.

EMERGENCY ROOM!

Preparation: Invite team members to bring their toughest challenges or problems to the meeting. Place an "Emergency Room" sign over the door and ask your most experienced team members to dress in medical garb and act as the emergency team.

Play: Team members take turns being called to the front to pose their problem to the emergency team, who will take turns prescribing a course of action that will fix it.

At the end of every meeting, team members will share their "What I will do" and "What I will stop doing" commitments. Follow up at the next meeting to see who kept their word and what improvements they have made to their business.

PARTY PLANNERS Ph.D.!

Preparation: Choose a chapter from *Be a Party Plan Superstar; Be a Network Marketing Superstar;* or *Be a Recruiting Superstar.*

Play: Base the content of your training on the chapter you have chosen, and ask team members to share one strategy they will commit to implementing in the month ahead. At the next meeting, invite them to share the difference it made to their business.

SUGGESTION BOX!

Preparation: Circulate a training topic to team members in advance of the meeting and invite them to bring their thoughts on that topic to the meeting. Ask them to place their idea in a suggestion box as they arrive, so that all contributions will be anonymous.

Play: Invite team members to take turns drawing an idea from the suggestion box and presenting it to the group.

Alternative: Invite newer team members to bring a challenge to the meeting and have them place it in a box. More experienced team members take turns drawing one out and recommending their best solution.

GAME SHOW!

Preparation: Use your creativity and imagination to adapt the theme of a popular television game show to train on a key topic (such as improving product knowledge).

Play: Invite one team member to dress up and act as the host of the show, and incorporate the theme, format, music, and phrases of the show into the enactment.

WHAT AM I?

Preparation: Write the names of a selection of products on separate cards.

Play: Team members take turns drawing a card and taking a seat at the front, where they will represent that product. Everyone else takes turns asking questions that will help identify the name of the product. No one can ask what the name of the product is, and questions can be answered only with yes or no. The first person to correctly guess the product represented wins.

PLAY FAVORITES!

Preparation: None

Play: Ask new team members to choose their favorite product and teach them the best way to present it:

* Focus on what the product will do (a benefit), not what it is (a feature).
* Share one key benefit and no more than two supporting benefits to avoid oversell.

*   Have them ask themselves, "Would my
     presentation make me want to buy this product?"
     and then adjust their presentation accordingly.

Give team members two minutes to prepare and thirty seconds to "sell" their favorite product to other team members.

Variation: Challenge experienced team members by allocating a product to them and giving them sixty seconds to formulate their sales pitch before presenting it to the group.

PART FOUR

When the Party's Over

CHAPTER 16

Time for the Reviews

THERE'S ONLY ONE WAY TO SHINE, and that's to keep polishing your presentations. If you plan on becoming a party plan superstar, you have to plan on making continual improvements to your parties.

Take a few minutes to review your performance and results after every party. These questions will help you evaluate what went well and what you can improve next time.

The first question to ask is, "Did I meet my attendance, sales, booking, and business targets?"

If the answer is yes, well done! But don't sit back and relax. You have proved you have what it takes, so your goal should be to *exceed* expectations. Increase your results and you'll increase your income.

The following questions will help you evaluate your strengths and weaknesses:

- ❑ Did I arrive, start, and finish on time?
- ❑ Did I bring everything I needed with me?
- ❑ Was I a gracious guest in my host's home?
- ❑ Did I give my host VIP treatment?
- ❑ Did I ask her to join?
- ❑ How happy was my host with her party?
- ❑ Did she say, "I'd be happy to do another party"?
- ❑ Did guests show an interest in my presentation?
- ❑ Was it alive with anecdotes and stories?
- ❑ Was I sharing new information and ideas?
- ❑ Did I welcome participation and interaction?
- ❑ Did I refer often to the business and the booking?
- ❑ Was I in control without being controlling?
- ❑ Did I try something new?
- ❑ Will guests be happy that they came?
- ❑ Did I spend one-on-one time with every guest?
- ❑ Did I try to up-sell?
- ❑ Have I sent thank-you notes to my host and guests?
- ❑ Have I added my host to my VIP Host Club?
- ❑ Have I added my guests to my VIP Customer Club?
- ❑ Have I recorded host leads I want to pursue further?
- ❑ Have I recorded business leads I want to pursue further?
- ❑ How happy am I with the party overall?
- ❑ What will I change next time?

Reviews are not intended as a "beat up" exercise. The only reason that you review your parties is to find ways to improve them. Small improvements add up to big improvements over time and each time you improve one aspect, even if it's a small change, you will move closer to your goal of being a party plan superstar.

Let your results do the talking. If your host promised ten guests and six showed up, take a closer look at your host coaching. She may have been a halfhearted or disorganized host, and she may have been affected by events beyond her control. But by playing the blame game, you relinquish control of your business to a third party. If you want to improve your results, don't expect others to change. You go first!

SUPERSTAR SECRET

Reviews are effective only if you can pinpoint the cause of your problems. If some guests slipped away before you took their order, was it because you forgot to ask, "Does anyone have to leave early?" so you could invite them to the front of the line for one-on-one time?

End your review by completing these two affirmations:

"Next time I won't . . ."

"Next time I will . . ."

Your reward will be in your paycheck.

CHAPTER 17

Follow Up

THE FOREMOST GOAL OF EVERY PARTY planner is to move as fast as possible beyond your inner circle of friends and family into new circles. A consistent party schedule is the surest way to make that happen.

The party is just the start of a relationship. Every guest is potentially a long-term customer, host, or team member. Your follow-up program is the key to turning casual customers into lifetime customers.

The more contact you have with your customers, the stronger the relationship will be. Over 90 percent of consultants start out as customers, so keep the lines of communication between you and your customers wide open.

Treat each guest the way you would like to be treated if the roles were reversed.

Send guests a friendly thank-you card no later than five days after the party, and remember to thank those who placed outside orders, as well as those who attended the party.

Make customer satisfaction calls a few days after guests have received their orders and say, "I can't wait to hear what you think." Ask if they have any questions and say, "I'm also calling to let you know that I'm sending you a 'Welcome to the VIP Customer Club' gift."

The second order is always the hardest one to get, so the best gift is one that will cost you only when customers redeem it, such as a voucher offering free shipping or 10 percent off their next purchase. Make sure the voucher has a sixty-day expiration date so you have a valid reason to follow up:

> "I remembered the voucher I gave you, and I wanted to make sure I called you before it expires. The timing is perfect as the hand towels that match the bath towels you bought are on special for the next two weeks."

> "We now have gorgeous new charms for the bracelet you bought. There's one that I think you'll especially love."

Don't hesitate to ask them again to host a party: "Now that you've had a chance to experience the products, how would you like to get your next order free? If you host a party you can stock up for nothing!"

To tempt them further, you may like to share what their host earned: "Julia's party was fun, wasn't it? I'm so glad you came. And she received over $100 worth of free products. It definitely pays to host your own party."

Don't forget to review the guest lists and call those who said they couldn't come to the party or didn't show. Offer these people a one-on-one consultation, or an invitation to your next open home or product launch, or send them to your Web site with a special incentive if they order online.

SUPERSTAR SECRET

When you call guests who didn't attend the party, say, "I'm sorry we didn't get to meet. You missed a great party but I saved you a small gift. If you would like a personal consultation, I can bring it with me. If you want to place an order now, I'll ship the gift with your products. Or you can host your own party and enjoy a free shopping spree. Tiffany received over $100 of free products so it's definitely worth it."

Building relationships is the key to direct selling. Never rely on your Web site or e-newsletter to service your customers. Making regular service calls will give you a chance to get to know your customers better, with your ultimate goal of turning them into hosts and consultants. Think of your earnings from the sales you generate as a bonus.

SUPERSTAR SECRET

Place five order forms next to your phone every morning, and when you call your customers, say, "I'm about to place my order. Is there anything you want me to order for you? The best offer this month is [name a product]."

Or you can say, "I'm offering my VIP Club customers 10 percent off their order [or free shipping or a free____] for the next twenty-four hours. Did you want to order the [name a product]?"

VIP Customer Club

Your VIP Customer Club will make your customers feel special and create the perfect vehicle for you to continue feeding information and offers about your products, bookings, and business to your best prospects.

Send members a monthly e-newsletter to keep your name, products, and business top of their mind. If you add a catchy headline, they will open it, and if you make it interesting with topical information, new ways to use your products, and exclusive specials, they will read it.

Think outside the box. If you sell food, cooking, or wine products, e-mail the following offer to your customers: "Do you belong to a club? Invite me to one of your meetings where your club members can enjoy demonstrations, taste tests, and samples and you can receive 10 percent of the sales in your own take-home goodie basket."

Your newsletter is not the only way you can make your VIP Customers feel special. Consider incorporating all or some of the following services into your VIP program:

* Special offers every month, featured in your newsletter or sent by e-mail or postcard

* A VIP Rewards Card (an electronic one will be easier for you both) that promises a free gift after five orders or for reaching a certain value of purchases

* Special invitations to your parties, product previews, and appreciation events

* Extra rewards for booking their own party

* Incentives for referrals

* Free samples in their orders

* A discount voucher on their birthday

* A birthday gift for the most active members

* Twenty-four-hours-a-day, seven-days-a-week ordering through your Web site to encourage your customers to order online

If geography permits, schedule customer care appointments

SUPERSTAR SECRET

Look for creative ways to drive your customers to your Web site, including:

* Run a customer-of-the-month lucky draw. All guests are eligible but they must visit your Web site to check for their name and to claim the prize.

* Post mystery prizes on your Web site and send clues by e-mail to help your customers and hosts find them.

and consultations with your best customers. An hour spent face-to-face with valued customers will strengthen your relationship, give you valuable insights into their lives, and tell you when and how to approach them about becoming hosts or consultants.

SUPERSTAR SECRET

Don't wait for your customers to contact you. Send surprise announcements on days when they are most likely to be home, for example, during storms, heavy snowfalls, heat waves, or holidays. If you're housebound, you can be sure others are indoors too, and will see your message as a welcome distraction.

Post specials and invitations on your Facebook page.

Don't send e-mails or Facebook messages when your customers are likely to be busy, as your message may get swamped in the incoming tide of e-mails.

You will increase responses if you include a link to an offer, such as double VIP rewards if they order from your catalog within twenty-four hours.

VIP Host Club

Your hosts deserve the highest level of attention and recognition. A VIP Host Club is the perfect way to make hosts feel special and appreciated and ease them into becoming consultants.

Immediately after the party, send your host a handwritten, thoughtful thank-you card that makes her feel good about her party and herself. You can never go wrong by looking for ways to compliment your host. The best way to make your hosts feel good about booking another party is to make them feel good about themselves.

Invite every host to join your VIP Host Club and enjoy special rewards, such as early-bird announcements about new products, promotions, and events; invitations to previews at your home; the first pick of dates; birthday gifts; exclusive specials; and extra gifts at their second and subsequent parties.

Think how special your host will feel when you say, "I usually invite my hosts to join my VIP Host Club after two parties, but your party was such a success [you were such fun to work with] I'm going to sign you up straight away."

 SUPERSTAR SECRET

Take a photo of every host at her party. Draw a "Host-of-the-Month" every month, send the winner flowers, and post her photo on your Web site for the month. It's all about the feel-good factor!

Invite every host to book another party when you have a good reason for her to do so: "We have a brand-new catalog and I can't wait to show you it. It has to be our best ever and I'm giving my favorite hosts first pick of dates."

When you contact hosts you haven't called in a while, you can say, "I've just realized I haven't called you to schedule a party this year. It's been crazy but I loved doing your party and we have exciting new products, plus a super special offer just for hosts for one month only. Are you ready for another party?"

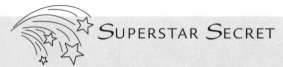 SUPERSTAR SECRET

When you have a cancellation, call a former host and say, "I had a last-minute cancellation so I thought, of everyone I know, who could throw a party at short notice? I immediately thought of you!"

A fun way to rebook your VIP Hosts and encourage VIP Customers to become hosts is to run your promotional booking month as an auction. Send out your available dates with the announcement that the first person to book each date wins a mystery prize, including the chance to win a $100 gift basket in addition to the regular host rewards.

Keep the business top of your agenda. Invite VIP Hosts to an "It Pays to Party" workshop, and tempt them with the irresistible incentives your company is offering while they enjoy VIP hospitality: "Join us on our next cruise to the Bahamas."

Be direct when you ask them to join: "I love doing your parties. I wish you would join my team. I think we'd have great fun working together."

Make it easy on yourself by devising a simple system for your host and customer care program. Your system could be as basic as creating separate folders for your servicing, booking, coaching, prospecting, and team support calls. Open each folder every day so you know what needs to be done in the different areas of your business.

 SUPERSTAR SECRET

You can safely assume that you won't be the only party planner approaching your host for a booking. Presenting your host rewards in new and exciting ways may tilt the booking in your favor.

Choose a busy or exciting month, such as your company's anniversary month, when your holiday catalog is launched, or when you need to jump-start bookings at the beginning of the year.

Call your VIP Hosts or send this announcement: "Next month, I'm celebrating by giving away $1,000 worth of free products to my VIP Club Hosts! All you have to do is book and hold a party in the next thirty days to participate in my biggest ever product giveaway!"

You can add to the urgency by saying, "The announcement will go out to VIP Club Customers tomorrow, but as a VIP Host, you have first pick of dates."

Much like the frenzy that happens when lottery organizers announce a big prize, the bigger the prize, the more people will want to be in to win. Your offer is sure to prompt many hosts to book a party.

How much will this cost you? Nothing more than you already spend on host rewards. Let's say your average host earns $100 worth of free products. Any month you do ten parties, you are already giving away $1,000 worth of free products. Nothing changes except the way you market your host plan.

Of course you must honor your promise and do enough parties to ensure that you give away the products as promised. But that's the easy part. Most likely your calendar will fill up so quickly you will have to open more dates for parties, or extend the promotion into the next month. It's all about creating excitement and presenting your host plan in an exciting way in order to attract bookings.

Note: Calculate the value of your giveaway by multiplying your average host reward by the number of parties you will do. A $100 average host reward multiplied by ten parties equals $1,000 worth of free products. If your average host reward is $50, promise $500 for ten parties, or do more parties.

However you choose to run your business, you must know that even your most loyal customers and hosts will eventually drift away if you're not regularly connecting with them. Relationships need contact to grow and develop. Make sure you communicate, communicate, and communicate.

SUPERSTAR SECRET

The sooner you go paperless, the more efficient, eco-friendly, portable, and profitable your business will be. Sending e-vites instead of postcards or e-mailing invitations by attachment so that your host can download and print them are good places to start.

CHAPTER 18

Share the Spotlight

YOU'LL FIND NO GREATER REWARD in party plan than being the catalyst for someone else's success.

No amount of money or recognition will eclipse the satisfaction you'll feel knowing that you played a key role in helping others achieve their goals. Seeing your consultants onstage receiving an award or on the gangway as they board their first cruise ship will always be a highlight of your leadership. Helping them blossom into leaders of their own teams will be both personally and financially fulfilling for you.

The highest rewards in party plan go to those who inspire and empower others to reach their true potential. Your ultimate success will always be directly linked to how successful your team members become. Duplication is the name of the game, and when you share your knowledge, skills, and experiences with your team members, your business will thrive.

When you reach the elite status levels of your plan, you will enjoy stupendous rewards. From a six-figure income to exotic travel, luxury cars, jewelry, gifts, and recognition, you will have it all when you master the Seven Golden Rules of Leadership.

Golden Rule #1: Walk the Talk

Here's your million-dollar question: "If everyone in your organization does what you're doing, what kind of business will you have?"

Every consultant you sponsor will have different expectations, circumstances, talents, and priorities. What they will have in common is that they deserve a leader who "walks the talk." The greatest demonstration of leadership is to be a shining example of how the business works and the rewards that come with success.

Your team members will do what you do. They won't do what you don't do. If you're not doing enough, or you're doing the wrong things, your mistakes will be compounded many times over, as your team members duplicate your efforts.

By leading from the front, you will light the path for others to follow. Your success will strengthen their belief in the business, in you, and in themselves.

When your team members see that you are spending half of your time on personal activity, they will recognize and respect you as a leader who walks the talk.

Golden Rule #2: Work the Numbers

The only way to keep your business firing on all cylinders is to fuel it with new people. The more consultants you sponsor, the faster you'll grow and the more relaxed you'll be about the revolving door that is party plan.

One of the most positive aspects of the industry's open-door policy is that we embrace a wide range of people. There is no discrimination based on gender, race, religion, experience, or education. Anyone over the age of eighteen can sign the Independent Contractor Agreement that gives him or her chance at success. Some will join with long-term dreams and some with small-time goals. A few will join on impulse with no set plans at all.

Whatever their motivation and however well you mentor them, some will perform a little, some a lot, and some will stall before they reach the starting gate. When you accept that the only security you have is numbers, you will make it a priority to sponsor a steady flow of new people.

New people breathe new life into your business and every one of them could potentially rise to team leader status, manager status, or higher. The more consultants who elevate, the faster you will elevate to the elite levels of your plan.

Golden Rule #3: Treat Every New Consultant as a Leader-in-Training

When you factor in the effort it takes to sign a new team member, the time you invest giving a person the best possible start makes good business sense. Surveys conducted by the Direct Selling Association show that half of all new direct sellers walk away from the business in the first three months. That's a huge amount of wasted energy spent bringing them into the business, as you are paid only on your team members' results. The sooner they start producing, the more they sell, and the longer they stay active in the business, the more you will earn from them.

Each new team member comes to you bursting with potential. You can never know how high they'll fly, but your belief, encouragement, and support as they navigate their first months will give them their best chance of success.

The relationship you establish at the start will set the scene for your relationship throughout, so make sure the commitment is mutual. If new recruits don't have a meaningful goal to work toward, and a commitment to the time needed to achieve it, they will drift like a boat without a rudder. Conduct a welcome interview to find out what they want to achieve and how much time they are willing to invest in their business. If you don't know what excites them, and how much time they plan to work, you will not be in a good position to help them.

Small goals are fine at the start. Many high achievers start with small goals that expand when they gain an insider's perspective of the business. Unrealistic expectations have a counterproductive effect. The fastest route out of this business is disappointment, whereas a series of small successes can lead to big progress over time.

At your welcome interview, help recruits understand the following:

* You will do all you can to support them, but their success will not be due to what you do, but what they do.

* It's okay to progress at the pace that's right for them. If they are willing to work and willing to learn, they will achieve their goals.

* There are no magic formulas and no shortcuts. Activity will drive their business, and the only way to learn the skills is on the job.

Here's an example of what to say:

"Lucy, I think you have incredible potential to make a success of your business. The best advice I can give you is don't underestimate your business because it cost so little to start. If you are willing to work and you're willing to learn, you can achieve anything you want.

"I know you can do it. If you hit a few speed bumps, welcome to the club. That's the learning process we all go through, and I'm here to support you all the way. All I ask in return is that you promise me you won't give up until you achieve what you set out to achieve."

The sooner new consultants start earning, the happier they will be. Nobody quits once they start making money, and even the most skeptical husband will come around when he sees the checks rolling in.

Having the first six to eight parties booked as soon as possible is critical to every new consultant's success, so schedule the Launch Parties as soon as possible and make sure you are there to support her. Your presence will provide a confidence boost, and you can keep an eye out for hot prospects in her inner circle whom she may overlook due to first-night jitters or familiarity.

It's your new consultant's time to shine so don't dominate the party but do ask to speak to her friends directly so you can convey this clear message: "I know you are all excited about Lucy's new business and we really appreciate your being here. The best support you can give her right now is to host one of her first parties. The good news for you is that the rewards you get for helping Lucy get started are incredible. Let me show you . . ."

Make sure you focus your new consultant on sponsoring from the start. Zoom in on her closest potential prospect by asking, "If you could take one friend with you on vacation, which friend would it be?"

Suggest that she invite that friend to join so they can support each other through their first few months. When two friends join together they both do better. New consultants may wonder if sponsoring will affect their sales. Reassure them that the opposite is true. The more people who represent their products, the more people will hear about them, start looking for them, and feel comfortable buying them.

Golden Rule #4: Give Clear Directions

Most new party planners have not been in business before and have to acquire the skills from scratch. If their expectations are realistic, they'll be emotionally equipped to stay the distance.

One of the greatest threats to new party planners' success is the small investment they made to start their business. When they hit their first sticky patch, they can walk away having risked nothing and lost nothing. To encourage new consultants to stay the course rather than drift away after a few setbacks, create a realistic roadmap for them.

Don't overwhelm them with information. Focus on what they need to learn *now*. As necessary as it may be for legal and ethical reasons, no one is going to be motivated by the policies and procedures manual or detailed explanations of the compensation plan. Focus on the products, the bookings, and the party. If your corporate manual is a blockbuster, recommend sections they should read first.

Make the corporate "Fast Start rewards program" their goal and their guide for their first three months. Every milestone

 SUPERSTAR SECRET

Support your new people through their first weeks by preparing a simple "cheat sheet" that lists training dates, coaching calls, and deadlines for their "Fast Start" rewards. Text a "Don't miss out" reminder a week before each "Fast Start" deadline and make a congratulatory call soon after they achieve it.

they achieve will strengthen their confidence in the business and themselves.

The first month will be their honeymoon period. They'll be swept up in the excitement and have lots of people to talk to. But they must learn how to transition from friends and family to a wider range of contacts. After thirty days, reality will set in and you must be generous with your time and your support. If they have mined their inner circle without generating a solid schedule of future bookings, they may begin to doubt the viability of the business, or themselves.

By monitoring their progress closely you will spot the red flags:

* If they're saying that "No one is interested/has the money/the time," they need help making calls. Chances are their enthusiasm is coming across as a sales pitch and they're not taking time to connect with their prospects.

* If they don't have forward bookings, they need training on how to expand their contacts. Most newcomers need help transitioning from their "warm list" of contacts to new people.

* If their party results are low, check that they are not making common mistakes:

    * Taking everything
    * Talking about everything
    * Focusing on the wrong things (e.g., the return policy)

Don't let seemingly small problems fall through the cracks. The sooner you fix small problems, the less likely it is they'll balloon into big problems. The longer you leave them unattended, the harder it will be to repair them.

Crunch time will come around the sixty-day mark. Some new consultants will be seeing real results and others may be struggling. If you have built a good relationship, you will know when to praise and when to gently suggest areas for improvement.

SUPERSTAR SECRET

Schedule an observation party with new consultants toward the end of their first six parties so you can see what's working well and where help may be needed.

Share your feedback with a "commend, recommend, commend" approach. If consultants feel good about what they're doing well, they will feel more confident about working on areas that need improvement. All feedback should start and end on a positive note.

Golden Rule #5: Be a Strategic Mentor

It's only natural for you to feel responsible for the consultants you sponsor. You introduced them to the business and you want the best for them. You also know that your success will be determined by how successful they become. But being self-employed means taking responsibility for your own success.

One of the greatest mistakes a leader can make is to work with the wrong people, and women are more likely to make that mistake. We are nurturers by nature and that can make us overprotective. But when someone you believe in fails to perform, making allowances, accepting excuses, or looking for ways to solve her problems for her is a surefire way to put the brakes on your business.

Some consultants will join with starry eyes but underestimate the amount of work involved or lack the drive and discipline it takes to be self-employed. It can be tough when someone you had high hopes for doesn't live up to expectations, but you must invest the bulk of your time mentoring new consultants and those who are producing results.

To put it bluntly, support those who deserve it, not those who demand it. Allocate the highest percentage of your time to new consultants and those who are producing. They are your future leaders.

Try to avoid the most common mistakes made by inexperienced leaders:

* *Giving parties to consultants who don't have bookings.* A consultant who can't create her own bookings is not going to learn anything from having them handed to her on a plate. Meanwhile, you have created two new problems: You have most likely destroyed the host's chance to earn booking credits, and you have squandered the leads that a skilled consultant could generate from the party. Your "generosity" will come at a huge cost.

* *Giving undue recognition to yesterday's performers.* Your consultants need to learn from role models who are actively working, and you're sending the wrong message by giving former stars influence or accolades they don't deserve. There are other ways you can show former contributors that you value them.

You may notice that the people who are doing the least are making the most noise. If you accept complaints or demands above performance, you're not doing your team members any favors. You're training them to dump their problems on you.

Just as the greatest gift you can give your children is the gift of independence, the greatest gift you can give your team members is to empower and equip them with the attitudes and skills they need to become independent managers capable of leading their own teams.

Golden Rule #6: Be a Proactive Manager

The greatest success in party plan goes to leaders who take a proactive approach to managing their business.

If you're a mom, or you're working another job with dreams of making your party plan business your sole source of income, time will be your greatest challenge. You're not going to have enough time to do the things you want to do, so don't waste time doing things you don't need to do.

If you're shuffling paper around your desk, chatting on the phone, or checking e-mails when you should be doing parties, coaching your hosts, and conducting sponsoring interviews, you'll be on a fast track to nowhere.

The only way you will build your business to the point where you can quit your day job is to ask, "What am I willing to give up in return for my dreams?" If you have to make phone calls during a lunch hour, miss a movie with friends, or resign from the school committee, do it! Don't waste time doing things that don't fit into your master plan.

No one has a greater stake in your business than you, so take responsibility for everything that happens, good and bad. People will sometimes let you down or fall flat on their promises. That's business and that's life. Party plan is a people business and that makes it volatile. But when you own the problem, you own the solution and that's leadership.

Let your results do the talking, and when something's not working for you, change it. No matter how much you want it, and how much you work at it, you won't grow if you keep repeating your mistakes. If you repeat them enough, even the smallest errors can sabotage your business big time.

Hold regular meetings at the same time each month and expect team members to attend. If you alternate live meetings with virtual meetings, there will be no excuse for nonattendance.

SUPERSTAR SECRET

Don't waste time creating training that is already available through other sources. Your leadership time is best spent on mentoring, not disseminating information. Consider yourself a resource center and direct team members to the best place to access the information they need when they need it.

Supplement your corporate training program with books and audio workshops from credible authors who have walked the talk and understand the challenges involved in building a party plan business.

Give new team members (or encourage them to buy) their own copies of *Be a Party Plan Superstar; Be a Recruiting Superstar;* and *Be a Network Marketing Superstar* to guide them. All three are available at most retail or online bookstores or my Web site, www.marychristensen.com.

For price savings on bulk copies, see the copyright page of this book for details on how to contact the publisher directly.

Monitor results every week so you know who is working and who is lagging and where to direct your energies. Don't be an end-of-the-month manager who looks at the figures only when it is too late to influence results. By keeping a close eye on performance, you will spot red flags, such as an emerging manager who hasn't placed an order by midmonth, so that you can intervene before the situation gets out of control.

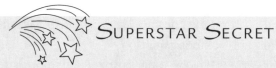

SUPERSTAR SECRET

Scheduling the bulk of your parties in the first half of the month allows you to spend the second half supporting your team.

Run your team promotions for the first three weeks of the month to encourage your consultants to follow your lead and ensure against end-of-month blues.

Golden Rule #7: Build Relationships

If you take care of your people, they'll take care of your business. Start by letting them know you value them as people, not just as producers. When you know what's going on in their lives, you will know how best to support them.

Make all team members feel involved and appreciated by planning a program that embraces everyone, from the lowest to the highest producers. There are many ways to do this:

* Share your vision. You won't be inspiring if you are not inspired.

* Keep their "why" alive by encouraging everyone to revisit their goals every year.

* Adopt a team name, and if you are a new leader, invite suggestions from team members and come up with the name together.

* Scatter a mix of business and social events throughout the year. Mobilize your troops from holiday to work mode with a lively jump-start meeting early in January, schedule a family picnic to unite the team through summer, and end the year on a high note with a celebration party.

* Promote one team, one dream. When your corporation announces the annual incentive trip, theme a meeting to fit the destination and encourage the whole team to

commit to qualifying. Be first to step up, by saying, "I'm going. Who's coming with me?"

❊ Create excitement with team "book-athons" and "spon- sor-athons" at key times to quick-start holiday bookings or launch a new catalog.

❊ Challenge your more competitive team members to beat their personal best and surpass your personal bookings, sales, or sponsoring results every month. You can be sure that some will rise to the challenge.

❊ Bring the team together to man a booth at a job or craft fair. You'll forge stronger bonds by planning and working the event together.

❊ Give your business heart by adopting a cause in your community. Invite your team to raise money to help a returned soldier, a child needing an operation, or a fam- ily who has fallen on hard times.

❊ Never be too busy to communicate on a personal level with a card on a team member's birthday or a call when a family member is ill.

❊ Be generous with praise and rewards for work well done. It's impossible to overstate the value of frequent calls and cards to recognize achievements and milestones.

❊ Make your meetings fun. If your meetings are dull, no one will show, or you'll forever be chasing down reluc- tant RSVPs. In Chapter 15, you'll find a wealth of games to pep up your meetings. Every meeting planner knows that the way to get people to come to a meeting is to host great meetings, and the key to great meetings is FIRE.

Fun!

Inspiration!

Recognition!

Education!

Make sure every meeting is a winning combination of all four components. If you focus solely on education at your meetings you will miss out on a perfect opportunity to build personal relationships and team spirit.

* Work hard to engage your team members when you're training by phone or they will quickly become distracted and inattentive. You don't want them to be folding laundry or checking e-mails when they're supposed to be learning.

* Don't rely on technology for all your communications. While your competitors are scrambling to find high-tech ways to make their lives easier, be the high-touch leader working the front line of your business, building and strengthening relationships with your customers, prospects, and team members.

* Take pride in maintaining harmony in your group. Even the slightest discord can have a destructive effect, and left unchecked could sabotage your business.

* Party plan is an emotional business. Fill and refill your team members with belief in their products, their business, and themselves, so no matter how often they are bruised by disappointments, delays, and downturns, there'll always be enough belief to see them through.

* Remember to acknowledge your team for the contribution they have made when you take the stage on awards night. Shared achievements build morale and strengthen loyalty.

* Above all, build fun into your business. Think back to the times you most enjoyed while you were growing your business, and work hard to create an environment where your consultants will feel included, involved, appreciated, and happy.

The good times will help balance out the challenges that are part of business growth, as it will take more than money to keep your team united through good times and bad. There may even be times when you'll hope your team members will step up to the plate for you, and that's when you'll need a big reservoir of team spirit and goodwill to call on.

It's Your Time to Shine

PARTY PLAN IS THE ULTIMATE VEHICLE for personal growth. It's practically impossible to grow a party plan business without growing yourself.

As you work toward becoming a party plan superstar, you will equip yourself with the skills of an elite business leader and inspire others to be the best that they can be. The more successful they become, the more successful you will become.

What draws women to party plan is that it is an equal opportunity, discrimination-free business. There is room at the top for anyone with the courage to dream big dreams and the discipline to see them to completion. What makes the business so special is that the only way you can fail is if you quit. If you are willing to work, willing to learn, and willing to stay the distance, anything and everything is possible.

This book has equipped you with the knowledge to become

a party plan superstar. It's time to apply what you have learned. There's no greater dream stealer than procrastination, and there's no better time than this minute to start transforming your life, one party at a time.

Start by refusing to allow forces beyond your control to undermine your destiny. Never give up on your goals, whatever happens in the economy or with challenges you face personally. Instead of waiting for the situation to get better, work on making yourself better.

The single most important ingredient in the recipe for success is courage:

* It takes courage to move beyond doubts and disappointments to pursue what you really want in life.

* It takes courage to walk away from a job that has passed its use-by date and to take responsibility for your personal and financial future.

* It takes courage to stop expecting others to improve and to focus on improving yourself.

* It takes courage to stop waiting for your circumstances to improve and to start focusing on improving your circumstances.

* It takes courage to move on from mistakes and focus on shaping your future.

* It takes courage to recognize when something is not working and to change it fast.

* It takes courage to refuse to let those who have given up on their dreams sabotage yours.

* It takes courage to keep moving until you achieve your goals, whatever setbacks you experience along the way.

* It takes courage to pay it forward so that others can follow in your footsteps.

✽   It takes courage to accept that you can't make excuses
    and money at the same time.

A meaningful goal + knowledge + courage + discipline =
party plan superstar!

Believing in yourself, believing in your business, and believing in your dreams will give you all the power you need to make
your dreams come true.

INDEX

More books for direct sellers by Mary Christensen

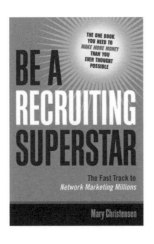

BE A RECRUITING SUPERSTAR

Everything you need to reach the highest income—a proven, innovative approach to recruiting that gets results fast.

BE A NETWORK MARKETING SUPERSTAR

Your step-by-step guide to becoming a direct selling superstar and living the life you dream about.